SALES PROMOTION DESIGN

SALES PROMOTION DESIGN

Robert B. Konikow

The Library
of Applied
Design
PBC INTERNATIONAL

Distributor to the book trade in the United States and Canada:

Rizzoli International Publications, Inc.
300 Park Avenue South
New York, NY 10010

Distributor to the art trade in the United States:

Letraset USA
40 Eisenhower Drive
Paramus, NJ 07652

Distributor to the art trade in Canada:

Letraset Canada Limited
555 Alden Road
Markham, Ontario L3R 3L5, Canada

Distributed throughout the rest of the world by:

Hearst Books International
105 Madison Avenue
New York, NY 10016

Library of Congress Cataloging-in-Publication Data

Konikow, Robert B.
    Sales promotion design / by Robert B. Konikow.
        p.   cm.
    Includes index.
    ISBN 0-86636-112-X
    1. Sales promotion.   I. Title.
HF5438.5.K67   1989
658.8'2—dc20   89-3438
                                                                    CIP

Color separation, printing, and binding by
Toppan Printing Co. (H.K.) Ltd. Hong Kong
Typesetting by **Jeanne Weinberg Typography**

10 9 8 7 6 5 4 3 2 1

CONTENTS

Trial

Programs emphasizing trade/consumer awareness and first time purchase

Intro by **Peter Yin**
Manager
Customer Automation
Marketing
Federal Express

Continuity

Programs developed to motivate the occasional buyer to become a steady long term consumer

Intro by **Joe Herrera**
Director of Marketing
Denny's Restaurants Inc.

Image/Awareness Enhancement

Events which reinforce a product's positioning in the marketplace

Display/Feature Ad Activity

Programs developed to generate the excitement necessary to obtain displays and trade merchandising

Intro by
Clifford R. Medney
Director
Sales Promotion
A&W Brands Inc.

Traffic

Events which emphasize the increase in consumer traffic at retail

Usage/ Consumption

Concepts which focus on greater usage of a product or service— extended use, off-season use, etc.

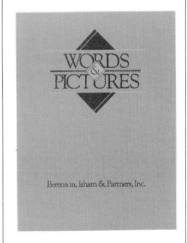

FOREWORD

Vincent Sottosanti
President
Council of Sales Promotion Agencies

Sales promotion has grown at an unparalleled rate over the past ten years, and today represents a major part of total marketing budgets. The future of the industry looks even brighter as the effectiveness of sales promotion proliferates in the companies that use it now, and its influence extends to more product and service categories.

Sales promotion, a critical factor in today's marketing mix, is distinctive as that element of marketing that is both action-driven and image-enhancing. Sales promotion can address one or all of the following objectives —and the list below is not necessarily complete:

- inciting sales
- building brand loyalty
- motivating the distribution chain
- attracting attention
- increasing awareness
- building traffic
- demonstrating product benefits
- generating trial.

Sales promotion's tools of the trade include sweepstakes/ contests; direct mail; point-of-purchase displays; meetings and conventions; product literature; premium/incentive programs; special events and celebrity endorsements; trade shows and exhibits; promotional advertising; audio/visual presentations; multi-company tie-ins; couponing/ refund programs; telemarketing.

As professionals, effective sales promotion is what we all strive for. This book recognizes some of the most interesting and effective promotions done in the past few years. It may well be an additional marketing tool to help each of us in our search for even better work.

Certainly, it will help the student and the cross-over professional better understand what it takes to be effective in today's marketplace. Too many companies, for too long, treated sales promotion as a second class citizen. Today, our industry is in the forefront. More people need to understand, and quickly, what sales promotion is about. This book will be extremely helpful in achieving this goal.

The companies whose work appears on the following pages are to be commended for the excellence of both the strategy and the execution associated in each effort. Most of the companies are members of the Council of Sales Promotion Agencies (CSPA).

Many of the promotions selected for these pages were screened by a panel of sales promotion professionals. So the judgments made were by a peer group of the people doing the work. We are also fortunate to see each of the six categories considered in this publication observed in some depth by the "men" who pay the bills. Surely, clients are a key critic in the evolutionary process of a campaign's effectiveness.

The Council of Sales Promotion Agencies is a dynamic, world-wide association of dedicated professionals. Over the past two decades, the dawning of the sales promotion industry has made a major impact on the inter-national marketplace. CSPA has emerged as the standard of excellence in sales promotion. Within the Council, CSPA ensures quality by providing direction and support to major agencies, nationally and internationally. Within the marketplace, CSPA defines the expanding role and impact of sales promotion. A voice for the industry, CSPA heightens awareness of the sales promotion profession.

Sales promotion professionals follow a methodical process to attain results. The flow begins with a thorough situation analysis—a determination of needs. It continues with the development of short-term and long-term objectives. Next, a strategy is devised to accomplish these objectives. The strategy must be on target; it must be consistent with the brand image; and it must be affordable within a given budget. Once the strategy is established, a creative execution and implementation of the promotion are carried out. Because sales promotion is measurable, it offers the opportunity for evaluation of results. At the conclusion of a project, the client and agency may compare the outcome with objectives and identify strengths and weaknesses of the program.

The opportunities and challenges facing companies in sales promotion will be enormous over the next few years. Those that deliver *effective sales promotion* consistently will be at the head of the class.

PREFACE

Working on this book, and reading and thinking about the case histories I have examined, both those that are included, and those that, for one reason or another are not, have left me with a deep respect for the creativity, the imagination, and above all, the professionalism of today's sales promotion practitioners.

In the early fifties, when, as a freelance writer, I started to produce articles on sales promotion topics for a wide variety of business magazines, I don't think we even used the term 'sales promotion' at that time. One of the magazines that used my articles was the Chicago-based publication, *Advertising Requirements*, which had started some time in 1952. In 1956, I became the magazine's Managing Editor, and in 1961, recognizing the growing integration of the media and techniques we were covering, we changed its name to *Advertising & Sales Promotion*.

It was during this period that the Sales Promotion Executives Association (SPEA), a group we editorially supported, was started. Later known as the Marketing Communications Executives International (MCEI), it was a struggling organization which just didn't make it. Nevertheless, it included among its membership and leadership some very fine people, many of whom I regard as friends.

In 1952, I left Crain Communications and A&SP to become a vice president and creative director of Abelson-Frankel, one of the new breed of sales promotion agencies. This gave me a new outlook on sales promotion, changing me from an observer to an active participant —a useful and educational experience.

After 2½ years at the agency, we parted company, and I returned to freelance writing and consulting, but I didn't leave sales promotion. My first and dearest client was the Exhibit Designers & Producers Association, for whom I acted as Public Relations Counsel. As part of this assignment, I became involved in the formation of the Trade Show Bureau, and acted as its PR Counsel during its formative years. At the same time, I began writing books, a number of them on aspects of both trade show exhibiting and point-of-purchase advertising.

But working on this book was like a return to familiar grounds, but with a fresh outlook, and it has been an interesting experience. I hope some of that interest is conveyed to you who are readers about and practitioners of sales promotion.

But this book couldn't have been done without the cooperation of people in the field, who have dug through their files to get the illustrative material we needed. In particular, I owe a debt of gratitude to the Council of Sales Promotion Agencies. The scheme of this book is based on the six categories which it set up for its 1989 Awards of Excellence competition. I also would like to thank CSPA for forwarding me copies of entries it had received. The decision on which to use, however, was mine alone, as are the descriptions of the promotions. Drafts of all case histories were sent to the submitting agency for comment and review.

Both the publisher and I would be very much interested in your comments on this book, descriptions of how you use it, and suggestions for making later editions more useful to you.

Robert B. Konikow

chapter ONE

Peter Yin
Manager, Customer
Automation Marketing
Federal Express

The Art and Science of Encouraging Trial

Getting consumers to try a new product or service is one of the biggest challenges facing the marketer. Initiating a trial is critical to the marketer because, obviously, the consumer must try a product or service before he/she can be convinced of continued usage.

Typically, individuals move through the following five stages of the sales process, also known as the adoption process:

Awareness: The individual becomes aware of the new product/service, but lacks specific information.

Interest: The individual is enticed to seek out information regarding the new product/service.

Evaluation: The individual evaluates whether the product/service will benefit him/her.

Trial: The individual tries the product/service to determine its value.

Conversion: The individual decides to become an ongoing user of the product/service.

Trial can be obtained through many devices. However, marketers rely mostly on promotion to generate trial. Advertising can also be used in conjunction with promotion to the consumer. It is also best to provide an offer along with a method to lead the consumer into conversion.

When developing promotional materials for a new product/service, marketers must keep in mind that individuals differ substantially in their willingness to try a new product/service. It is natural that some individuals are more willing to try new products/services in each product area than others.

For example, some computer engineers are more willing to try a new technological computer versus some who have never used a computer. Individuals can be categorized into adopter categories as shown in the following chart[1]:

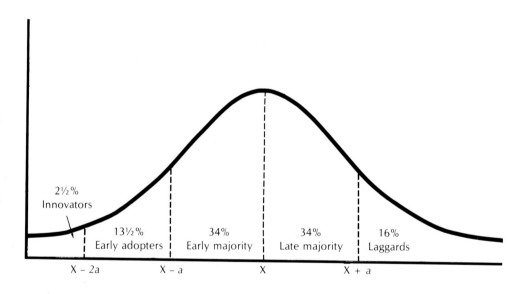

Time of Adoption of Innovations

This chart represents the percentage of individual willing to try a new product/service, after a slow start.

Innovators are trend setters; they are willing to try almost anything at some risk. *Early adopters* are cautious triers. The *early majority* is faster to try a new product/ service than the average person. The *later majority* is real cautious; they only try a new product/ service after they obtain trial, because advertising is an excellent vehicle to generate awareness.

The following promotional tactics can be used to obtain trial:

Sampling—Providing the individual with the product/ service to try. Sampling is usually free.

Free with purchase—If the individual buys product "x," he/she will receive a free sample to try the product/service.

Premiums and incentives—If the individual tries the product/ service, he/she will be given a gift or rebate. This is an incentive to try.

Couponing—Offering a discount for the individual to try the product/service.

Introductory pricing—Introducing the product/service at a discounted price to entice trial.

Special packaging—Special packaging to create curiosity in the individual to try the product/ service, or using the two strongest words in promotion— FREE or NEW—to create curiosity.

The tactic, or what direct mail people call the offer, that a marketer uses depends on his/ her target market. Before creating an offer, the marketer must examine his/her markets' likes, dislikes, needs, interests, and so on. The offer must also be in character with the product. For example, if the product is a serious one, so must be the offer. A marketer will obtain a higher rate of trial if the offer is simple and doesn't confuse or create apprehension. *Laggards* are very skeptical of change. These individuals only try a new product/service if they have to.

In summary, trial is critical to the marketer because a consumer must try a product/service before becoming an ongoing user. There are several promotional tactics that a marketer can choose in order to gain trial. However, the marketer must know the target audience before developing the promotional tactic.[2]

High Tech
Needs High Design

CLIENT:
Cinch Connector Division,
Elk Grove Village, IL
(Bob Marker)

AGENCY:
Mark Anderson Associates,
Arlington Heights, IL
(Jim Hanson)

When you're dealing on the frontier of technology, you've got to look it. All the materials you use to tell the world about your product must reflect the high-tech approach. In this promotion, the product is a miniature connector used in the manufacture of computers. How miniature it is may be seen from the photograph of a dime, which holds half a dozen or more of the tiny connectors.

After naming the product and designing its logo, the agency set up a brief tour to demonstrate its features to the editors of the three most important technical publications in the industry. These presentations were given in the offices of the magazines and were attended by their editorial staffs. The client's technical people, of course, did most of the talking, but representatives of the agency accompanied them.

To show the details of these tiny products, a series of slides was used. These illustrated the special characteristics of the connectors, pointing out how the designers had achieved objectives that had eluded earlier technicians.

Press kits were available to leave
behind with all editors in attendance. These included stats of the key
technical and application slides used
in the presentation, as well as other
reference material. These were contained in a custom-designed folder
which used a dramatic four-color
photograph on its cover. These visits
to key editors were successful, for
all three of the publications ran a
feature article on the new product.
After these initial presentations, a
press kit, much like the one that had
been used in the personal visits, was
sent out to the client's entire media
list.

A four-page, full color capabilities
brochure was added. Additionally, a
product sample folder and a design
guide was also included. At the same
time, the initial slide presentation
developed for the press tour, was
transferred to video, and will be
used as a sales tool and as a teaching
aid to educate salesmen.

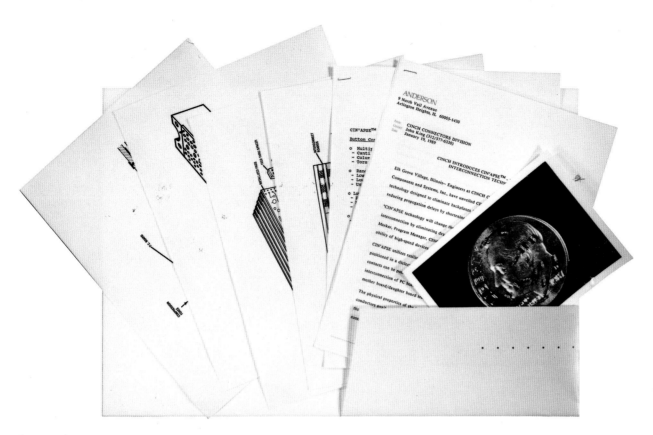

The press kit included the dime photo, as well as a number of line drawings that showed both the details of the connector as well as its applications.

The array of dots symbolizes the connector, and is used consistently on all printed pieces, even on this qualifying business reply card that accompanies responses to requests for literature.

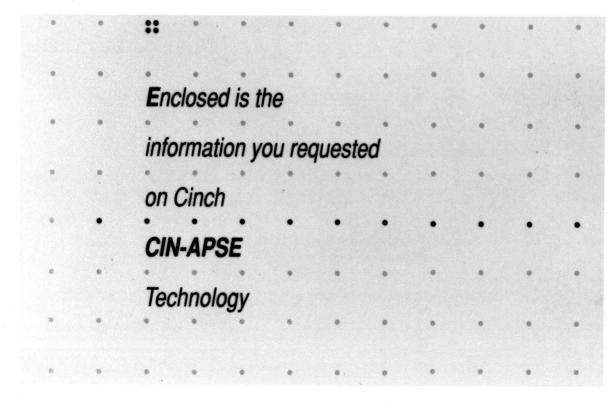

Enclosed is the

information you requested

on Cinch

CIN-APSE

Technology

CIN∷APSE

A **N**ew **P**atented **T**echnology

Bringing **PC** **I**nterconnects

Up **T**o **S**peed

CINCH

A Division of Labinal Components
and Systems, Inc.

The cover and inside spread of the product brochure used the dots that symbolize the product.

CIN•APSE™ Approaches Ultimate

Connectivity–Significantly Reduces

Propagation Delays

Build a Promotion around a Photo

CLIENT:
W.H. Brady Co., Thinfilm
Products, Milwaukee
(Joe Michaud)

AGENCY:
Mark Anderson Associates,
Arlington Heights, IL
(Jim Hanson)

AWARDS:
Electronic Components News'
Ad-Chart Award, December 1988

There are times when a good photograph can serve as the thing that ties a promotional campaign together, and this is a good example of this approach. What Brady was selling was a process, a new way of applying a variety of thin-layered materials, precisely controlled, upon flexible substrates. The end result was not a brand new product, but was an improved one, more reliable and more economical than those produced on hard or tough film substrates, using earlier techniques.

The photograph was, of course, in color. It showed, on the left, an example of the thin film coating typical of many applications. The dark background of the photo made it possible to use headlines and text in dramatic reversal.

The photograph was used as the basis for a full-page ad that ran on a six-time schedule in the leading publication that reached the electronics designer audience which made production decisions.

It also served, without the ad copy, as the cover of a gatefold folder that was used in a number of ways—in response to inquiries produced by the advertising, as a leave-behind piece, and as a press kit. This folder, large enough to handle a standard sheet of paper in its pocket, carried two pages of explanatory copy and illustrations. The left-hand page, using five illustrations, talked about the properties of the film and its manufacture, while the right-hand page, with its three color shots, discussed specific applications. These photographs were also used in mail-outs of five individual product releases, and in the development of five product-specific advertisements, which was a good utilization of existing photography.

The back cover of the folder used text and two diagrams to explain how the process worked, and its advantages over existing procedures. All in all, in minimum space, it told the entire story of the process.

After the first year of the program, more than 3,000 sales leads have been generated, at a cost, for the entire program, of less than $75,000.

THE PATTERN OF THINGS TO COME

Thin**FILM**
Sputtered Web Coatings

A Breakthrough in Thin Film Roll Coating Technology

The new Bradyflex™ family of thin film products is evidence of the breakthrough Brady has achieved in patterning thin film sputtered web coatings onto flexible plastic substrates.

Utilizing our continuous web or roll-to-roll thin film manufacturing processes, we have developed a broad line of Bradyflex™ products which are inherently economical and provide innovative solutions to challenging product design requirements.

Through unique manufacturing processes and state-of-the-art analytical instrumentation, Brady's Thin Film Products organization is committed to pioneering patterned thin film coatings on flexible polymeric materials—*the pattern of things to come.*

Creating Superior Thin Film Coatings Through Sputtering Vacuum Deposition Processes

The sputtering process is simply described as a vacuum deposition process whereby the application of a negative electric potential to a sputtering target contained within a vacuum chamber creates a plasma or glow discharge. Positively charged gas ions generated in the plasma region are attracted to the negative potential at the target and propelled towards it at very high velocity. The subsequent collisions between the positively charged gas ions and target result in a momentum transfer to the target surface atoms, and ejection of atomic size particles out of the target. These particles traverse the vacuum chamber and are deposited as thin films onto the surface of the substrate material.

Sputtering is the preferred vacuum deposition technique for the production of high quality thin films on flexible webs or rolls. Thickness uniformity is excellent in both transverse and longitudinal directions. When compared to thin films deposited by evaporation, sputtered films are extremely dense, and possess superior electrical properties and adhesion to the underlying materials. Sputtering is also a more flexible process. It is possible to produce alloys of precise composition by conventional sputtering, and oxides, nitrides and other compounds by reactive sputtering, where an additional reactive gas, such as oxygen or nitrogen, is introduced during the sputtering process.

Sputter Roll Coating Process

Web sputtering is an efficient method of applying uniform thin film coatings to large surface areas on flexible substrates. Brady's sputter roll coater can deposit high quality thin film coatings of metals, alloys and/or compounds such as oxides and nitrides, in single or multiple layers. Special features include sophisticated process monitoring, glow discharge substrate surface pretreatment for improved film adhesion, and unique patterning capabilities.

Sputtering Vacuum Deposition Process

Thin Film Sputter Roll Coater System (Cross-Section View)

BRADY

W. H. BRADY CO.
THIN FILM PRODUCTS

The cover of a sales brochure was later adapted for use as the press kit cover.

Bradyflex™ Transparent Heaters are designed for numerous industrial applications such as heating backlit liquid crystal displays.

Bradyflex™ Thin Film Flexible Opaque Heaters are lighter, thinner and more flexible than conventional etched foil heaters.

Bradyflex™ Cu raw materials have varied electronic applications such as adhesiveless TAB tape for advanced packaging of semiconductor devices, high density flexible circuitry, and EMI/RFI shielding.

Features of Brady's Thin Film Sputtered Web Coatings

These are just a few of the many benefits inherent in Bradyflex™ Thin Film Products:
* Pattern Metallized thin film coatings on flexible plastic substrate materials. * Capability to selectively deposit dissimilar materials on same plane or level. * Multilayer single-or double-sided thin film coatings. * ± 5% thin film coating thickness uniformity. * Reactive sputtering processes (oxides, nitrides, etc.). * Glow discharge substrate pretreatment. * Up to 20-inch web width and production of sheeted parts up to 20" x 20". * Base substrate films of Mylar® polyester (PET) and Kapton® polymide. (Other materials available upon request.)

Note: Mylar® and Kapton® are registered trademarks of the E.I. DuPont De Nemours & Co., (Inc.)

Superior Sputtered Web Coatings Technology Provides Outstanding Production Benefits

A few of the unique benefits Bradyflex™ products provide include:
* Lower material/component costs * Increased design and production flexibility * Space and weight reduction * Increased flexibility * Enhanced functionality * Increased product design freedom * Easy surface mounting of electronic components directly to thin film coatings * Excellent adhesion of thin film coatings to the underlying base substrate * Extremely dense coatings.

Bradyflex™ Flexible Circuitry products offer many advantages such as weight reduction, greater flexibility, and the ability to surface mount components directly to thin film conductors.

Brady's sputtered Thin Film web coating technology has many electronic component applications such as keyboard cores and membrane switches.

BRADY.

Bradyflex™ ITO materials can be used in ESD Static Dissipating applications such as the cover tapes used on surface mount device carrier tapes.

Brady Thin Film Products Organization's Unique Manufacturing Technical Capabilities

From conductive inks and die-cutting to over-laminates, precision slitting and sheeting, the Thin Film Products organization offers a variety of adjunct manufacturing and technical capabilities. Pressure-sensitive transfer adhesives, printed or roll coated adhesives, and protective (hard) coatings further enable us to create the thin film product your application requires.

Brady's Product Quality and State-Of-The-Art Analytical Capabilities

Each thin film product we produce is designed and manufactured to the most stringent specifications. Brady utilizes a complete array of state-of-the-art analytical instrumentation to ensure the highest standards of quality for its thin film Bradyflex™ products.

Outstanding Customer Service

The long-standing W.H. Brady Co. tradition of outstanding customer support is continued by the Thin Film Products organization. Providing our customers with the finest capabilities and service is the goal of every employee. We invite you to call us today, so that we can begin working together on the challenges and opportunities patterned thin film coatings will present in the future.

Bradyflex™ multilayer transparent thin film coatings can be designed for use in anti glare optical filter and EMI RFI TEMPEST shielding products for CRT screens.

Bradyflex™ ITO patterned transparent electrically conductive materials can be employed in the manufacture of touch sensitive electronic input devices.

BRADY.

The basic photograph as it was used in the trade ad.

The two inside pages of the folder, with their illustrated explanations of the process and its uses.

A little larger, and with less type, the photograph serves as the cover of the explanatory folder.

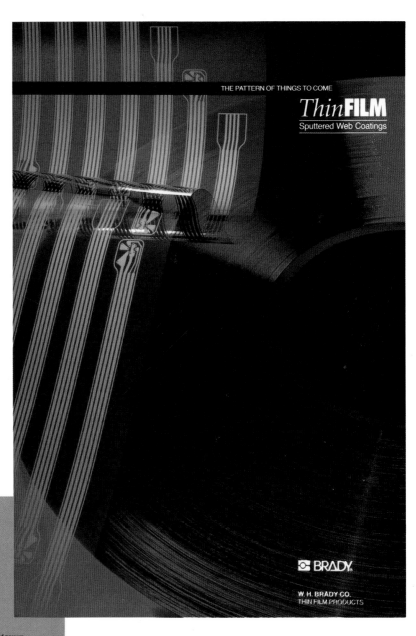

A Breakthrough in Thin Film Roll Coating Technology

The new Bradyflex™ family of thin film products is evidence of the breakthrough Brady has achieved in patterning thin film sputtered web coatings onto flexible plastic substrates.

Utilizing our continuous web or roll-to-roll thin film manufacturing processes, we have developed a broad line of Bradyflex™ products which are inherently economical and provide innovative solutions to challenging product design requirements.

Through unique manufacturing processes and state-of-the-art analytical instrumentation, Brady's Thin Film Products organization is committed to pioneering patterned thin film coatings on flexible polymeric materials—*the pattern of things to come.*

Creating Superior Thin Film Coatings Through Sputtering Vacuum Deposition Processes

The sputtering process is simply described as a vacuum deposition process whereby the application of a negative electric potential to a sputtering target contained within a vacuum chamber creates a plasma or glow discharge. Positively charged gas ions generated in the plasma region are attracted to the negative potential at the target and propelled towards it at very high velocity. The subsequent collisions between the positively charged gas ions and target result in a momentum transfer to the target surface atoms, and ejection of atomic size particles out of the target. These particles traverse the vacuum chamber and are deposited as thin films onto the surface of the substrate material.

Sputtering is the preferred vacuum deposition technique for the production of high quality thin films on flexible webs or rolls. Thickness uniformity is excellent in both transverse and longitudinal directions. When compared to thin films deposited by evaporation, sputtered films are extremely dense, and possess superior electrical properties and adhesion to the underlying materials. Sputtering is also a more flexible process. It is possible to produce alloys of precise composition by conventional sputtering, and oxides, nitrides and other compounds by reactive sputtering, where an additional reactive gas, such as oxygen or nitrogen, is introduced during the sputtering process.

Sputter Roll Coating Process

Web sputtering is an efficient method of applying uniform thin film coatings to large surface areas on flexible substrates. Brady's sputter roll coater can deposit high quality thin film coatings of metals, alloys and/or compounds such as oxides and nitrides, in single or multiple layers. Special features include sophisticated process monitoring, glow discharge substrate surface pretreatment for improved film adhesion, and unique patterning capabilities.

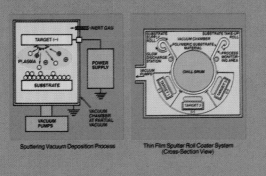

Sputtering Vacuum Deposition Process

Thin Film Sputter Roll Coater System (Cross-Section View)

The technical explanation page that appears on the folder.

Challenging the Leader

CLIENT:
George Dickel Tennessee
Whiskey

AGENCY:
Focus Marketing Inc.,
Norwalk, CT

AWARDS:
1989 CSPA Award of Excellence
(Finalist)

It's hard being number 2 or even number 3, especially when you believe—and when blind taste tests back you up—that you should be number 1. But that's the situation with Dickel Tennessee Whiskey, whose sales run behind both Jack Daniels and Jim Beam, the big guns in the bourbon industry. What can you do about it? Dickel decided to challenge the leader by building a campaign around blind testing, involving as many consumers as possible. It was attempted, even though it is not easy to get involvement in the hard liquor industry. In this case it was done in fun but with a serious objective.

A totally integrated year-long promotion was developed under the banner of the "Dickel Duel." The central characters of the promotion were two mythical duelers, named "Jack" and "George" after two not-so-mythical brands. Their duel was, of course, over the taste of the two brands, and bourbon drinkers were to be given a chance to compare the tests of Dickel and its competitors.

The "duel" and its accompanying blind taste tests were carried out at all levels. Dickel salesmen challenged on-premise bartenders to a duel, in an effort to persuade the professional drink dispensers that there is a real difference in taste. Bartenders can be influential in recommending a brand, and often make the decision when the customer does not specify a brand.

On special bar nights, the duel is expanded to involve customers in blind taste tests, in events conducted by members of the beautiful "Duelettes." These evenings are promoted in advance, and they help bring customers onto the premises; although the test tastes occupy some of those present, additional volume is produced. Most importantly, brand preferences are often changed when a steady user of one of the competitive brands finds that, when he can't see the label, he often prefers the taste of Dickel's.

Taste testing cannot be done, of course, in off-premise stores, but the concept can be and was indeed promoted. The main component was a pair of life-size cut-out figures of the dueling men. These combined with a stack display of Dickel whiskey produced a traffic-stopping display. In conjunction with this display, the consumer was offered his own "Dueling kit," complete with marked glasses, bar towel, and other necessities.

The final phase of the dueling campaign was to schedule events around the country where press people were invited to "duel." To date, 80% of the journalists who participated picked Dickel!

The campaign is working. The initial order of display and other materials has been consumed, and a second printing has been ordered. What is more important, sales of Dickel's Tennessee Whiskey have been increasing. The brand, a product of the Schenley American Whiskey Group, has shown a double-digit percentage increase since the promotion started. And, this in a category of the liquor industry that has been declining.

Two life-size cut-out figures, each with a drink in one hand and a weapon in the other, made a stack display floor stand.

The colorful sell-in brochure issued the challenge with the slogan "May the Best Whiskey Win."

May The Best Whisky Win

Sales Will Be Smokin' All Year Round

Ain't nothin' better than an eye-catching display to get folks in the mood for sippin' Dickel. And there'll be plenty of sippin' goin' around with the George Dickel Duel and Tasting Kit Offer.

GEORGE DICKEL
Tennessee Sippin' Whisky

...AY
...l be buying George Dickel by the
...r. This authentic whisky barrel
... down home spirit of George
...ld-fashioned refinement.

DICKEL SALOON
Customers will stop on by this Fall for at least one bottle, at this authentic George Dickel Saloon Display.

CODE # GD-423

Increasing
Consumer Response

CLIENT:
Ore-Ida Foods Inc.

AGENCY:
The Niven Marketing Group,
Scottsdale, AZ
(Ron Macsenti)

Ore-Ida is the leader in packaged frozen potatoes, but while leadership helps introduce a new product, you can't rely on consumer acceptance of the company name alone. So when Ore-Ida was ready to introduce its Toaster Hash Browns, it wanted to do it in a way that would build trial purchases and increase sales.

Working with its sales promotion agency, it decided to use a full-page free standing insert, but instead of utilizing the typical tear-off coupons, it attached a consumer response card to the cover of the insert. While use of this technique with other products have been shown to increase customer response by as much as 200 percent, Ore-Ida decided to test it. It utilized a split run with the response card in a portion of its national market, and a standard coupon in the remaining areas.

Point-of-sale materials featured a die-cut toaster with a visual of the product and the sales message. A special, full-color folder was prepared to introduce the new product to the trade.

Early tabulations show a substantial increase in redemption when the response card was used, compared with the rates achieved by the standard couponing method.

The sell-in brochure used a photograph of a freezer case packed with the product.

Promotion
to Build Knowledge

CLIENT:
Thomson Consumer Electronics
Canada Ltd., Mississauga, ON
(Graham Thorpe)

AGENCY:
The Promotion Core, Toronto
(Shirley Ward-Taggart, Peter Van
Vlaardingen, Ina Harrison, Gladys
Bachand, Paula Kerr)

It's an unusual promotion that is based on product knowledge, and that runs over a long period, and here's an example of one that worked—and worked well. While RCA is a leader in the electronics industry, there is always room to upgrade an image, and reward sales. So when it decided to develop an awards program for its dealers, it wanted one that was unique to the industry, that presented itself in a prestigious, upscale manner, and that could judge the overall effectiveness of its dealers.

Working with its agency, The Promotion Core, a division of Leo Burnett, RCA developed a two-year program that would be based, not only on sales, but also on a total understanding of RCA and its activity in the marketplace.

The first year of the program was built on the heritage of the famous RCA dog and gramophone symbol. Under the banner theme of The Golden Gramophone Awards, a prestigious golden brochure and entry booklet were sent out to all RCA dealers. Dealers were asked to answer questions regarding product knowledge, point-of-sale, advertising, promotion, and store sales/audit informaion. Each dealer had from August until March to fill it out, and to include photos of displays, newspaper ads, radio scripts, and videos of that particular store's promotional activity. Entries were scored on a point system to arrive at

60 semi-finalists, 10 finalists, and one grand prize winner. Semi-finalists received certificates of achievement. The finalists received a small sculptured award of the RCA dog and gramophone plus a trip to the Bahamas. The grand prize winner was awarded a trip to Hong Kong, along with a large Golden Gramophone award.

RCA's own internal sales force also competed in the program, but with different criteria, to win Certificates of Achievement, plus a trip to the Bahamas.

The first year, the competition drew 345 entries, representing 46 percent of all RCA dealers in Canada. Such a return was considered enormously successful—so successful, in fact, the competition was held a second year, but this time with some additional embellishments. In addition to a booklet outlining the terms of the competition, each retailer received a videotape extolling and elaborating on the event. The incentive to participate the second time was a grand prize trip to Australia.

Dealers from all parts of Canada participated, from small town stores to large warehouse-style outlets. The quality of the entries, and the effort put into them, was surprising, proving that the dealers took tremendous pride in their product knowledge and in-store displays.

Both dealers and RCA sales reps indicated a high level of awareness of the promotion. Since the Golden Gramophone Awards program provided a means for RCA to build a premium quality image as well as to measure dealers' performance, RCA expects the program will evolve in tandem with its place in the highly competitive electronics industry.

GOLDEN GRAMOPHONE A WARDS

The first annual 1988 Golden Gramophone Awards celebrated crowning achievements, in The Bahamas.

Creativity and initiative set the winners apart.

Judging for the Awards was based on four principal criteria:

- presentation of new RCA point-of-sale material
- merchandising of top-of-the-line RCA brand models
- quality of co-op advertising
- quality of special promotional activities

For the 10 finalists of The Golden Gramophone Awards, April 21 to 24, 1988, capped off a year of hard work and effort.

To salute their accomplishments, the following 10 finalists were rewarded with an exclusive watch, a unique Golden Gramophone Award, plus 4 fabulous days in the glorious Bahamas.

Congratulations to each and every member of the following Thomson dealerships:

Blairmore Radio & TV
Blairmore, Alberta

Brunelle Electronique
Coaticook, Quebec

5th Avenue Electronics
Lethbridge, Alberta

Gordon's Radio & TV
Dauphin, Manitoba

Happy Video
Richmond, British Columbia

John's Electronics
Chilliwack, British Columbia

Lounsbury Compagnie
Lemeque Island, Quebec

Petrie TV and Appliances
Weston, Ontario

Saskatoon TV Centre
Saskatoon, Saskatchewan

Trio Home Furnishings
Duncan, British Columbia

At the gala dinner, the Grand Prize winner was announced: Trio Home Furnishings of Duncan, B.C. The Golden Gramophone Award included a fabulous 2-week Cathay Pacific Discovery Tour for 2 to the Orient, plus $1000 in spending money.

Lorne Campbell, National Sales Manager, presents the prestigious 1988 Golden Gramophone Award Grand Prize to the National Winner: Charlie Erickson of Trio Home Furnishings, Duncan, B.C.

Celebration in The Bahamas went beyond the Awards. It included a celebration of friendship and comraderie associated with being an RCA dealer and part of a network on the move.

It was also a celebration recognizing individual contribution to Building Trust Through Customer Service. Claude St. Germain was singled out as Sales Rep of the Year, and Rick Daly as Zone Manager of the Year.

Now is the time to start preparing for the 1989 Golden Gramophone Awards, because next year we'll do it all again.

Thomson Consumer Electronics Canada, Inc.

Congratulations!

®Registered Trademark of RCA Inc.

The second year's promotion was introduced with a special videocassette. A golden folder included the rules of the contest and the forms that had to be filled in to qualify.

Appealing to the Man within the Man

CLIENT:
Skoal/U.S. Tobacco Co.,
Greenwich, CT
(Joe Bertolas)

AGENCY:
Bell & Partners, South Norwalk,
CT
(Martin J. Bell)

Chewing tobacco is a man's product, especially Skoal, a product of U.S. Tobacco Co., the leader in the moist tobacco industry, with a five-year growth trend that's up 41 percent!

This promotion built on the image of the Skoal user, who tends to be a blue-collar worker, between 25 and 49. He is a man who rolls up his sleeves, isn't afraid of a hard day's work, often works with his hands so that he can't always smoke, and dreams of being his own boss.

Skoal was ready to encourage this dream by inviting men to enter a sweepstakes with a first prize of a $100,000 White GMC Truck, plus $20,000 in cash. This prize would be enough to set up the winner as his own boss, an independent truck driver. There were 15 second prizes of full sets of Goodyear Eagle tires, and 1,000 third prizes of leather-bound Rand McNally Atlases.

To enter the sweepstakes, all one had to do was to pick up an entry blank at a retailer, and use it to request a free pack of Skoal from the manufacturer. The form had some questions to add to U.S. Tobacco's database, with information about whether the individual was a first time user, used Skoal or another brand, and whether he currently owned a truck.

While Skoal is sold at many places that handle tobacco products, truck stops are a major outlet for this product, and the advertising and promotional material was concentrated there. In addition to advertising in national and regional magazines that appeal to this audience, space was purchased through Pica, which owns a nationwide network of display cases in truck stops.

Point-of-purchase was installed through the sales forces of both U.S. Tobacco and its distributors. This included window posters, riser cards and pre-packed 24-can displays, both of the latter carrying sweepstake entry pads.

To encourage participation by retailers, special promotional allowances were offered for the period of the promotion, as well as a sweepstakes in which the first prize was a $50,000 White GMC short conventional truck and customized body.

Over one million entries were received at sweepstakes headquarters, which was just under 3 percent of the total coupon impressions produced, and one-third of them requested samples. A high percentage of these were first-time users, thus meeting one of the promotion's primary objectives. The popularity of the promotion with retailers was indicated by the fact that over 100,000 pre-packed, 24-can displays were achieved.

The sell-in brochure shows the grand prize, in all its might, on the front cover.

ROLLS INTO TOWN

The SKOAL MAN Sweepstakes is set to roll into town with an opportunity for someone to win the key to a whole new way of life. The grand prize – a WhiteGMC Heavy Duty Truck – means one lucky person will win the unique chance to head out on the road for himself and become his own boss.

SKOAL LONG CUT* – A Product that Moves in the Fast Lane

- U.S. Tobacco is the established leader in the moist smokeless tobacco industry – with a five-year growth trend that's up 41%!*
- The largest sweepstakes promotion ever sponsored by U.S. Tobacco, with total prizes valued at over $150,000:
  – Grand Prize – WhiteGMC Heavy Duty Truck + $20,000 cash
  – 15 second prizes – full sets of Goodyear Eagle tires
  – 1,500 third prizes – leather-bound Rand McNally Road Atlases

Heavy Traffic Accelerates Profits

- National and regional print advertising – with a total readership of 95,741,000 – will pull customers into your stores to:
  – buy Skoal Long Cut
  – pick up sweepstakes details, entry forms
- Increased traffic means increased sales – and increased profits – across the board.
- Prominent POS materials designed to stimulate impulse purchases for greater sales, higher profits.
- Sweepstakes entry forms offer free samples of product with bounce-back coupon to generate additional sales down the road.

*THE SKOAL MAN and SKOAL LONG CUT are trademarks of United States Tobacco Company.

*1986 Maxwell

Sweepstakes Tear Pads
- contain entry forms for sweepstakes
- offer consumers free product samples and bounce back coupons

National and Regional Print Advertising
- Total Readership over 95 million
- National publications include TV GUIDE, FIELD AND STREAM, POPULAR MECHANICS and SPORT.

Riser Cards and Window Posters
- Increase consumer awareness
- stimulate impulse purchases

The last page of the brochure shows other promotional items offered to the retailer.

THE SKOAL MAN* SWEEPSTAKES
24-can Promotional Display Package

- Pre-packed display package contains 24 cans of Skoal Long Cut* with six cans each of:
  - Wintergreen • Straight
  - Mint • Classic
- UPC:
  Promotional Display Package 73100-00079
  Promotional Case 73100-00080

*THE SKOAL MAN and SKOAL LONG CUT are trademarks of United States Tobacco Company.

Order Information:

One of the sheets inside the brochure illustrates the pre-packed counter display.

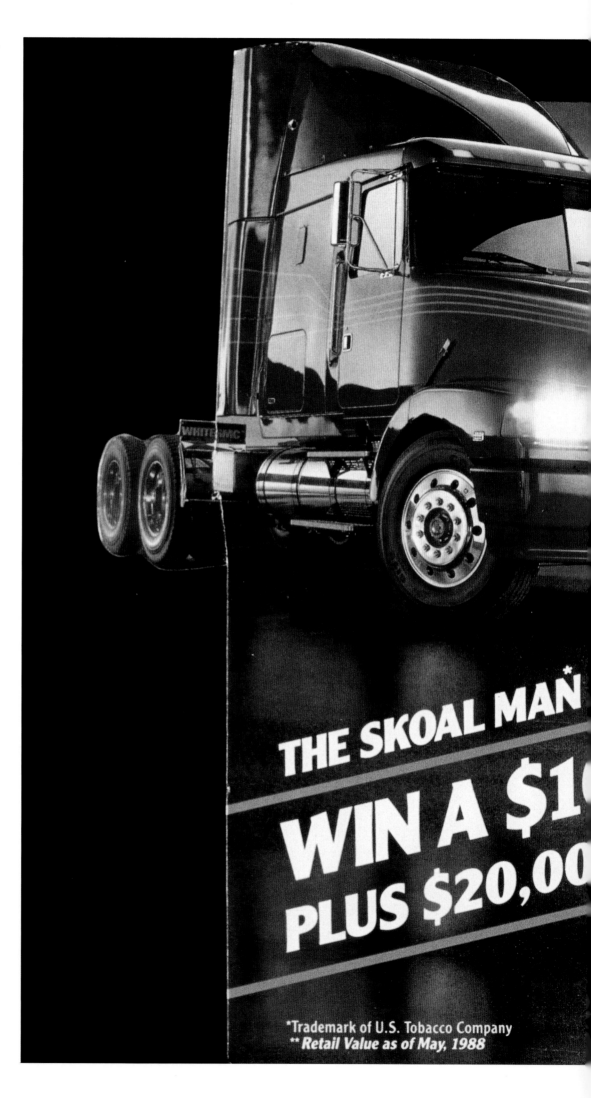

This riser card carries a pad of tear-off entry forms.

THE SKOAL MAN*

WIN A $1

PLUS $20,00

*Trademark of U.S. Tobacco Company
** *Retail Value as of May, 1988*

A Coach is a Coach

CLIENT:
Thomas Built Buses,
High Point, NC
(Ron Moore)

AGENCY:
The Downs Group Inc.,
Charlotte, NC
(Kirby Strickland Sr., Tyler Glenn,
Rob Jamison, Chuck Royer)

AWARDS:
1988 B/PAA International
Pro-Comm Award
1989 ICITA Award
1988 PICA (Printing Industries of
the Carolinas)
1989 Carolina Chapter B/PAA
Pro-Ad Awards

It isn't often that a promotion can be built around a play on words, but when it can be done, it may be very effective. That was the case when the product was a school bus, or a coach, being promoted to school systems, in which a coach is often a very important person. The wordplay that developed led to some interesting mailings in this three-part campaign.

Thomas was introducing its MVP™ Rear-Engine Coach to the school market, and it wanted to attract the attention of specifiers and purchasers of school buses, to arouse the interest of those currently seeking to purchase school buses, and get them to identify themselves, so that personal contact could be made with these potential buyers. The answer was a mailing campaign of three pieces, each sent to a carefully-developed mailing list.

All three pieces were similar in design. Each was a brightly-colored flat box: the first green, the second blue, and the third red. Each contained a slogan in white type on the lid, with wording that suggested the gift inside. The copy picked up on the slogan, while a business reply card was there if the recipient wanted to have more information. Each package was sent approximately four weeks apart.

The first box carried on its green cover "Blow the whistle on buses that aren't true coaches...," with the inner heading "Insist on a real coach—a SAF-T-LINER MVP™." The gift was a coach's whistle on a lanyard.

The slogan on the second mailing was "Don't buy a school coach till you've tried an MVP™ on for size..." The inside head continued "It fits all your safety needs with room to spare." The gift was an extra large navy blue T-shirt with a white stylized bus, the Thomas logo, and the letters MVP in white on the back.

The third mailing, in the red box, carried the slogan "Make a heads-up play, and put an MVP™ into your line-up...," and contained a white coach's cap, with the letters MVP embroidered on it, just under the Thomas stylized bus logo. If the recipient allowed his friends to think that MVP stood for Most Valuable Player, who would deny it? The lead-in to the copy carried out the theme with the words "No substitute scores as many points for cost-efficiency..."

The direct mail campaign was part of a complete communications program that included publicity, trade publications advertising, product literature, and a product video. According to Thomas, the MVP campaign has been its most successful product introduction ever, a tremendous success with sales more than doubling expectations.

They're

Introducing Thomas' SAF-T-LINER® MVP™ coach. The one without the kinks. The one you've waited for. The one for your valued passengers.

With Rear-Engine Advantages.
It protects passengers better in rear-end collisions. It eliminates driver distractions

from heat, noise, and dangerous fumes. And the three-door, easy-access engine compartment allows faster servicing.

Extra Fuel-Tank Protection.
The tank's nestled between chassis frame rails, and also enclosed in a steel cage. That's solid protection from rear, side, and front collisions.

Out.

Thomas Quality And Construction. Important safety features include our extra-strength body and roof. And there's an unexcelled warranty on body and chassis. Full information is in the new MVP™ brochure, free from us or your Thomas distributor.

SAF-T-LINER MVP.™ It's a true coach. Rear-engined. Sized for 60 to 78 passengers. And priced just a bit above competitive-styled buses. The wait's over.

1408 Courtesy Road, High Point, NC 27260 U.S.A., Woodstock, Ontario, Canada Quito, Ecuador, S.A.
Phone 919/889-4871

Thomas Built Buses®

...a tradition in transportation

Three square boxes, each with a
three-dimensional gift, made up the
direct mail series.

The single-page ad ran in leading
school bus publications for a couple
of months as a "teaser" to inhibit
the purchase of competitive coach
buses.

Before You Spec Another Bus, Make Sure All The Kinks Are Out Of It.

Choice: You can rush out right now and buy an unproven light-duty transit-style bus, and regret it. Or wait just a bit for Thomas' new SAF-T-LINER® MVP.™ And be satisfied.

It's a true coach; its engine is in the rear, for greater safety and easier maintenance. SAF-T-LINER® MVP.™ Lower-capacity, priced right, and it's coming out soon.

Thomas Built Buses®

...a tradition in transportation

45

Before You Spec Another Bus, See The New-Size Coach Called MVP™!

Here's a true rear-engine coach that's affordably priced!

Introducing the SAF-T-LINER MVP™ by Thomas. A true coach, with the engine in the rear. A true Type-D design, with important safety and servicing advantages. But because it's a lower-capacity configuration, it comes at a lower price than the large coaches.

MVP™ — True collision protection. The rear engine is ideally positioned to absorb impact in a rear collision, to help protect passengers.

And the fuel tank is located behind the front axle, between extra-strong frame rails, inside a tough steel cage. That's solid protection from rear, side, and front collisions.

True coach, truly good price. Considering all the advantages of this new bus, you might get the idea that MVP stands for Maneuverability/Visibility/Protection — or maybe it means Most Versatile Performer. Either way, we're confident you'll consider it a Maximum-Value Purchase — a school or activity bus that's sized right and priced right!

Safety and quality features make the MVP™ your best coach value!

You compare:

1. **Monolithic Galvalume™ Steel Floor**
2. **Special Fuel Tank Shielding**
3. **Extra Heavy-Duty Frame Rails**
4. **Roof Coach Rails**
5. **Efficient Rear-Engine Design**
6. **Removable Rear Frame Bumper**
7. **Engine Location**
8. **Outside Access to Electrical Control Box**
9. **Full Out-and-Opening Doors**
10. **Exclusive "Circle of Safety"**
11. **Premier Protection Plan™**

SAF-T-LINER® MVP™

SAF-T-LINER® MVP™...True coach features, but sized smaller — 60 to 78 passengers — and at a lower price than the large coaches.

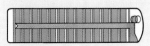
78 passengers

72 passengers

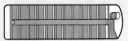
66 passengers

60 passengers

Engine:	Detroit Diesel 8.2N, 170 HP Detroit Diesel 8.2T, 180 HP, turbo-charged Caterpillar 3208N-200 HP, except in California
Transmission:	Allison AT545 automatic
Front Axle:	11,000 capacity
Rear Axle:	19,000 capacity
Front Brakes:	15.0" x 4.0"
Rear Brakes:	16.5" x 7.0" "S" cam type
Fuel Capacity:	60 Gals. (between chassis frame rails)
Suspension:	Leaf springs front and rear; 30,000 maximum (depending on tires)
Steering:	Power, Ross model HFB64
GVWR:	30,000 pounds (depending on tires)
Passenger Capacity:	60 to 78 (subject to weight limitations)

Thomas Built Buses®

...a tradition in transportation

1408 Courtesy Road, High Point, NC 27260
Phone: 919/889-4871
Woodstock, Ontario, Canada
Quito, Ecuador, S.A.

United Way

We reserve the right to discontinue or change the specifications or design at any time. Some options and accessories shown in this brochure may be at additional cost.

SAF-T-LINER is a registered trademark, and MVP and E.R. are trademarks of Thomas Built Buses.

TO81/988

Multi-position steering wheel is an available option, to help adjust driving controls to individual drivers.

Caterpillar's naturally-aspirated 200-HP 3208N diesel engine is available. (N/A in California)

Driver's area of the SAF-T-LINER® MVP™ is designed for more visibility and comfort, less distraction.

Detroit Diesel's naturally-aspirated 170-HP and turbo-charged 180-HP engines are offered everywhere, including California.

Rear-engine design provides flat, clear walkway for easier, safer entrance and exit (no engine-compartment cover in floor).

Easy access to electrical control box trims servicing time, costs.

A product brochure went into the technical advantages of the new bus.

To Get Money,
Use Money

CLIENT:
Mellon Bank East, Philadelphia

AGENCY:
Saatchi & Saatchi Promotions,
New York
(Robert Petisi)

The banking industry in Philadelphia is highly competitive, although a substantial one. CDs alone total about $13 billion, and this is growing at more than 3 percent per year. Mellon Bank East holds the fifth position in CD sales, yet is has only a 4 percent market share.

To encourage people to open CDs at its institution, the Mellon Bank adopted two strategies. The first was to develop a new kind of certificate, called the Flexible CD, offering customers advantages not available at other banks. In addition, it set up an exciting new sweepstakes, open only to those who took out new CDs during the promotional period.

Entering the sweepstakes was deliberately made easy. In fact, the consumer didn't need to do anything beyond opening a new account, or rolling over a maturing one. For every $500 a consumer deposited or rolled over during each week, he or she automatically received one entry in the sweepstakes. No entry form was needed, the bank's computer was programmed to award points to each depositor, and to make the random selection for prizes.

Three hundred and two prizes were awarded each Monday, all of them cash. One depositor received $10,000 as the first prize, another was chosen as the second prize winner, for $4,000, while there were 100 third prizes of $100, and 200 fourth prizes of $50.

The promotion was announced via local print and radio advertising. In addition, there were simple displays developed for use in the 74 participating branches. Counter cards called attention to the contest, and folders which spelled out the rules and the awards, as well as the special features of the Flexible CD, were distributed at the teller windows.

Originally scheduled for six weeks, the contest proved so popular that it was extended an additional three weeks, bringing it very close to the 1988 Christmas holidays. A total of $34,000 was given away each week, amounting to a prize structure of $306,000.

The copy didn't change, but a variety of sizes were used on posters and counter cards to spread the word in the bank's branch offices. Radio and newspaper advertising were also part of the program.

Even the Best Idea must be Sold

CLIENT:
Federal Express, Memphis
(Peter Yin)

AGENCY:
Frankel & Company, Chicago
(Pam Church)

AWARDS:
1988: Certificate of Merit, Direct
Marketing Association Tempo, 1st
place, Chicago Association of
Direct Marketing
1989: Award of Excellence (Best
of Category), Council of Sales
Promotion Agencies
Gold Medal (Best of Category),
SPIRE, American Marketing
Association.

Federal Express had a problem: Business was booming. You don't think that's a problem? But more business meant more customers calling for pick-ups, and more calls meant more people to handle the growing volume of calls, and that meant that it would have to build and staff additional call centers.

A quick study of the budget for increasing call centers led to the conclusion that the investment was too great, and that some other technique must be developed. The system that Federal Express turned to was a custom-designed, high-tech process, in which a customer could dial a toll-free number and, without taking the time of an agent, enter his request for a pick-up, using touch tone entry. These telephoned requests, using customer account numbers for identification, were quickly forwarded to the appropriate Federal Express office.

The system worked well—test calls placed via touch tone were promptly and accurately forwarded. The only problem was that customers weren't using it. It was announced in five cities, but calls did little more than trickle in. People were simply not using the service, either because they had failed to read or understand the announcement letter, or because they were reluctant to rely on the new system. Something had to be done to move people.

At this point, Federal turned to Frankel & Company and asked for a promotion that would encourage a customer to use the new service instead of calling an agent. Frankel suggested a direct mail campaign using the tag line "We've Got a Great Pick-Up Line."

The campaign had to have wide appeal, since the people to be moved by it, the people who were to be persuaded to use this new way of getting a pick-up, varied from mailroom personnel to top executives. The first mailing came in a quiet envelope, of unusual shape and size—9"x 9¼"—with the tag line printed in red just above the address window. The major element was a replica of a touch tone telephone, forming a pocket. The instrument section slid out of the pocket to give directions on using the new Federal Express number. A card in the envelope held a die-cut Rolodex card, giving the FedEx number, plus the customer's account number and the zip code at the pick-up spot, information that would be needed when placing a call for pick-up. The upper half was a business reply postcard, which the customer could use to keep track of the times the service was used, with a place to jot down the authorization number of each call. When four calls had been noted, the customer just dropped the card in the mail, and the premium of an imprinted coffee mug, along with envelopes of instant coffee and tea bags, would be sent out. A sample tea bag and coffee packet was also included in the first mailing. Since this mailing was sent only to regular users of the service, there was little or no waste circulation.

The main incentive for customers to utilize this new way of asking for a pick-up was, of course, its simplicity and its ease of use, saving the user valuable time. But the special premium that was offered for systematic use of the new service helped get customers in the habit of utilizing it. The coffee mug had "I've got a great pick-up line" on one side, and a FedEx logo and its 800 telephone number on the other. It was filled with individual coffee and tea packs, and was free with four usages of the service.

Did this plan work? The trial calls in the first city to get this mailing out-numbered the five-city introduction by more than 500 percent, with more than 50 percent of the recipients of the mailing using the new system. The special premium offer, based on repeated use of the system, was earned by more than 16.6 percent of the mailing recipients.

The system has been introduced, market at a time, and after more than a year in this phase, the call volume is exceeding the number of mailings sent by more than 25 percent. Although the system is not yet available in all markets, the estimated daily savings to Federal has already exceeded $10,000!

Federal Express is thrilled. Customers are pleased (one woman even went out of her way to call to find out who developed the promotion package); the campaign continued to be effective as the system was introduced into each of Federal's market cities.

The first mailing, in a large, nearly square envelope, contained directions, a convenient Rolodex card, and a return postcard to send in when the service had been used four times.

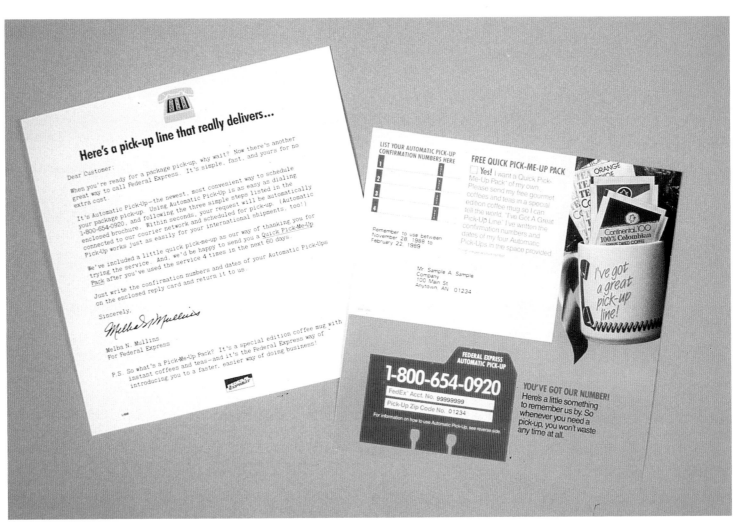

For using the service 4 times, the customer received an imprinted coffee mug, filled with packets of coffee and tea. It is shown here with the mailing that explained the offer.

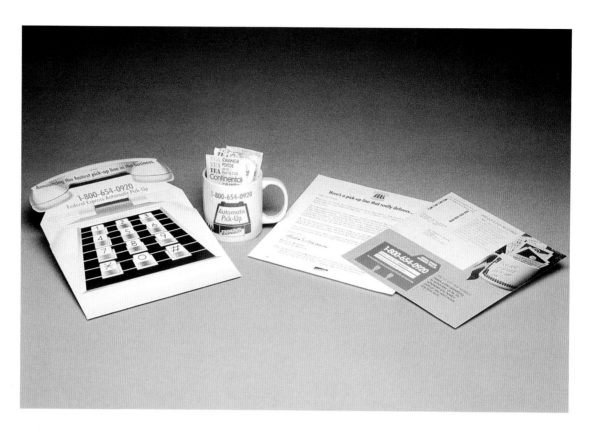

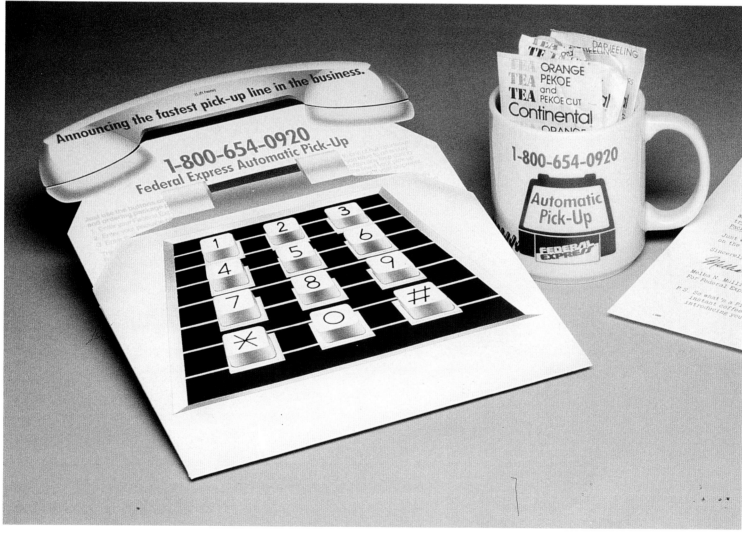

Promotion in the Van

CLIENT:
Nestlé's Foods, Confection
Division

AGENCY:
Promotional Innovations,
Stamford, CT
(Jim Zembruski)

When you're selling a product that depends on satisfying the taste of customers, getting them to taste the product is the best way to build acceptance. Many ways have been utilized to make it easy for people to taste a new product. Samples have been sent through the mail, and have been attached to regular packages of a brand that has the desired customer profile. Coupons and trial-sized packages have encouraged the purchase of a product without making a major investment in an unknown package.

But Nestlé's, working with its sales promotion agency, Promotional Innovations, has developed a new technique—a fleet of specially-painted vans. These unusual vehicles have been used to promote five brands of candy—Crunch, Chunky, Oh Henry!, Raisinets, and Alpine White.

Each side of the vehicle is painted with a design built around one of the five logos, so that the van is, in effect, an outdoor bulletin on wheels. Another logo is used on the other side to build versatility into the program.

The vans could be sent anywhere there were enough people with the right demographics to match those of the brand. Alpine White, for example, is positioned against upscale males and females, while Oh Henry! consumers are typically teens/young adults 12-24.

The vans were used at a wide variety of events. They were, of course, frequently parked outside supermarkets that were willing to cooperate by offering product display and increased shelf presence. They also appeared at such events as fairs, baseball games and other sporting events, or anywhere people gathered. Tie-ins were arranged with radio stations and other major trade factors.

The drivers would give away samples and/or coupons. They could also conduct games involving the product, and redeem wrappers for premiums. The effect of the vans was apparent; they helped to increase trade merchandising activity, like displays, shelf placement and brand mention on trade/radio station tie-ins. They built consumer traffic as a result of their appearances, and increased consumer purchases via their participation in premium give-aways of such articles as T-shirts.

Each of the vans was painted differently, according to the candy it was promoting.

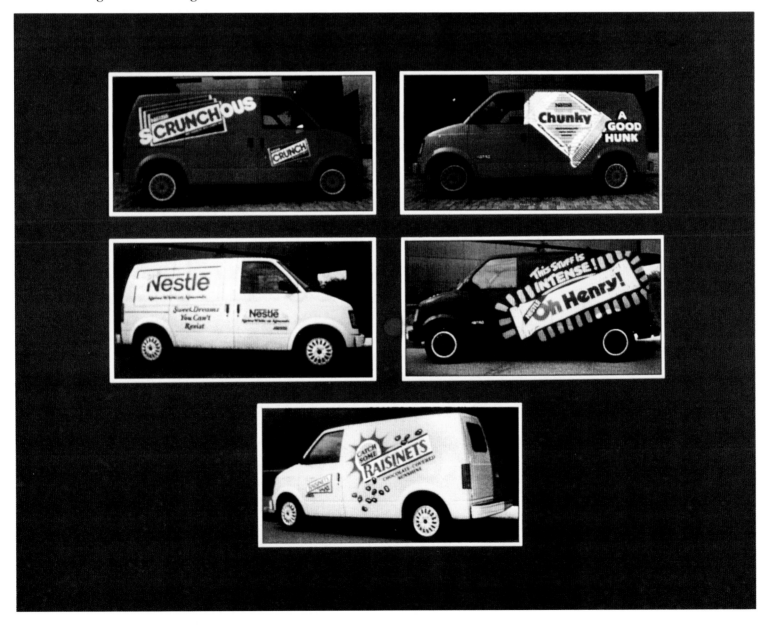

Promotion is More Important than Position

CLIENT:
Forbes Steel & Wire Corp.,
Canonsburg, PA
(Ed Lawther, Pete Dichuk)

AGENCY:
Giltspur Exhibits/Pittsburgh
(Judi Baker-Neufeld)

AWARDS:
Gold Medal/Leads, Direct Mail
Category, 1989 Sizzle Award

What do you do when your product isn't very glamorous, when you have only a small space, a poor location, and a display that hasn't been upgraded for years? The answer is that you identify your key prospect group, recognize their needs and interest, and make your booth a "must see" on their list.

Forbes Steel & Wire Corporation manufactures welded wire structural fabric which is used in reinforcing concrete slabs, replacing the more familiar reinforcing bars. The company was assigned a small, 10' x 10' booth, in a remote corner of the large World of Concrete, a major trade show that attracted 750 exhibitors and 17,500 visitors. But only 900 of these were specifiers and buyers of the Forbes fabric, and it was these people that had to be attracted to the booth. While this audience was small in numbers, it had large buying power for Forbes' product offering. The company would be satisfied with an opportunity of talking to only 50 of this 900.

To emphasize the primary product benefit of time and cost savings, the pre-show promotion strategy was communicated through a time clock image. The clock represented a critical element in major construction projects. Saving time and beating the clock translated into increased profits for the contractor.

Instead of doing an extensive job of upgrading the exhibit, Forbes decided to focus its efforts on a creative pre-show mailer with a contest tie-in, and a comprehensive post-show reinforcement package administered through a lead management service to provide effective response to prospect inquiries, and timely reports to its sales force and management.

The mailer came in a 6½" square envelope, with a picture of a time clock immediately setting the theme. The illustration was repeated on the cover of the folder. When the recipient opened the folder, he saw a miniature time card coming out of the time clock's slot. This card served as a registration card at the booth, with a floor plan of the show on the reverse, showing the location of the Forbes booth.

On show-site, blow-ups of the time clock art with product benefit bullet points added, were displayed prominently in the booth. The panels provided quick identification of the exhibit for target prospects. When they arrived at the booth, invitation in hand, they were met by Forbes people, who completed a booth staffer/lead card on each attendee. If they had technical questions, there were qualified experts on hand. In any case, the lead cards were entered into a drawing to win a "Beat the Clock" digital travel alarm clock. In reality, all qualified prospects who returned their cards to the booth received the clock.

The lead cards were shipped daily by air express to the Giltspur Lead Management Center in St. Louis for next day distribution of the appropriate fulfillment materials. Lead notices and summary reports were provided to Forbes a week after the close of the show. The prospect packet included an updated catalog, the contest gift, a conversion reference table, and a letter of appreciation from Forbes management.

While 50 qualified leads were expected, the actual response was a total of 103 qualified leads from the show floor, with additional responses from non-attending prospects.

Forbes Steel PreShow Mailer and Premium

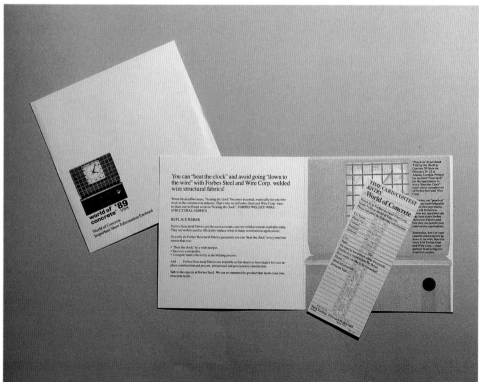

Each prospect who turned in his time card at the booth received an imprinted travel clock.

The square invitation, stressing the time clock, got prospects thinking right away about the benefits of saving time.

Forbes Steel-Post Show Fulfillment Package

A special folder, with literature developed specifically for this purpose, was included in the packet that went to booth visitors.

Selling Service with a Smile

CLIENT:
Rochester Telephone Corp.,
Rochester, NY

(Rosanna Garcia)

AGENCY:
Pierce Brown Associates,
Rochester, NY

(Patrick Shirley)

The Rochester Telephone Company was about to introduce a number of new services to its patrons to make the average phone more adaptable to many different lifestyles. These features included customized ringing, in which three different telephone numbers can be received on one phone line, with each phone having a different ring; three-way calling, which allows you to talk to two people at the same time on the same line; call forwarding, which permits you to forward all your calls to a predetermined number; and call answering, which is an automated answering service.

While promoting these new features, Rochester Telephone wanted to enhance its public image, to be seen as more of a communications partner, and less as a stuffy public utility. To break the stiff image, its advertising/sales promotion agency suggested a program that used interesting visuals, unusual headlines, and humorous radio copy to catch the attention of the target audience. While the features had their own built-in interest, the agency felt that a public utility that "let its hair down" would garner more attention.

The first item in the campaign was a bill stuffer. Rochester Telephone was dubious; it felt that bill stuffers were never read, just thrown away. However, it was persuaded by the agency's arguments, and agreed to try it.

The stuffer was a simple folder with a headline that was bound to get attention, especially in an envelope delivering a monthly bill. It read, in large reverse type, "Blanche Loves It!" and the inside spread was headed "So Does Don." What Blanche and Don loved, one learned from the inside of the folder, was Call Answering and Call Forwarding. Starting in the middle of November, and running for five weeks, the stuffer was included in the normal billing cycle, reaching a total of 383,000 consumers. RT projected a response of 34-38 percent, but actually received a much higher response by the end of December, even though the mailing cycle ran right into the hectic holiday schedule.

Two other media were used in the campaign: newspapers and radio. Both tried to present their messages in an honest, straightforward way, but not with a stuffy demeanor. The newspaper ads, each 9" x 14", covered all aspects of the new services, using simple headlines and unusual illustrations.

The five one-minute radio spots were all informal dialog, each illustrating the use of a single feature with a somewhat humorous approach. In talking about the phone with a different ring for each member of the family, the story was told with a racing background, as family members unnecessarily raced for the phone. The script about call forwarding took place in a police station, where a woman was reported missing because her friend could never reach her on the phone. The situations were exaggerated, but they still told the story in a somewhat tongue-in-cheek manner.

Blanche Loves It!

Get new Custom Calling Features— you'll love them!

RochesterTelephone

So Does Don.

❝I do a lot of volunteer work. And with Call Forwarding and Call Answering, I don't have to sit home waiting for my calls. People who need me can reach me fast. It saves me time—and I love not missing any calls!❞

Blanche Johnson, Greece resident
and community volunteer

❝In my business, you can't afford to miss phone calls...can any business? Call Forwarding and Call Answering help keep my day on schedule, and I don't miss important calls. Great flexibility—I even use these features with my car phone.❞

Don Cameron,
Rochester insurance executive

New Custom Calling Features...for the way you live your life.

These days, it pays to take advantage of whatever makes your life easier, like Custom Calling Features. They're convenient, affordable services you can add to the telephone you already own!

Call Forwarding

This feature lets calls reach you wherever you go...so you never have to miss a call. All you need is a telephone!

Call Forwarding—Busy

When your own line is busy, this feature automatically forwards incoming calls to another prespecified number. It's a great alternative to missing those important calls.

Call Forwarding—No Answer

Here's a feature that automatically forwards incoming calls to another prespecified number when no one is available to answer your telephone.

Call Answering

This Rochester Telephone service uses a recording of your voice to take messages whenever you don't answer your phone. And you can retrieve those messages from *any* touchphone, anywhere.

Wouldn't *you* love Custom Calling Features? Call for more information and pricing today—**777-1200** (Residence) or **777-1234** (Business).

Not all Custom Calling Features are compatible.

The original bill stuffer attracted a high rate of response, even in the busy pre-Christmas season.

Look at what your phone can do now.

Custom Calling Features make your life a little easier.

Busy, busy, busy. That's the way life is for most people these days. Custom Calling Features help take the busy work out of your busy day. Your phone can do a lot more than sit there and ring. You can take it easy with these services:

Call Waiting–A soft tone lets you know a call is waiting. Use Cancel Call Waiting for those times when you'd rather not be interrupted.

Call Forwarding Features–Put an end to the old telephone run-around. Call Forwarding routes your calls to any phone so you don't miss a call. Call Forward–No Answer lets calls reach you at a designated number when you can't get to the phone. Call Forward–Busy automatically forwards your calls when your own line is busy.

Call Answering–Forward your calls to this automated message service so you'll never miss a call. This convenient feature stores messages until you're ready to retrieve them.

Three-Way Calling–You can talk to two people at the same time, around town or across the country.

Speed Calling–Save time and use one or two digits to dial frequently called numbers.

Customized Ringing–When the phone rings, you'll know who the call is for. You can get up to two additional numbers, each with its own distinctive ring, on your existing phone.

Make it easy on yourself. For more information or to order any Custom Calling Feature call **777-1200** (RESIDENCE) or **777-1234** (BUSINESS).*

RochesterTelephone
For the way you live your life.

*Subject to availability.

Put an end to the old telephone run-around.

With convenient Call Forwarding features, your phone calls follow you wherever you go.

Stop the frustrating game of telephone tag with our trio of Call Forwarding features.

It's like being in two places at one time.

It's a win-win situation for you, your friends and business associates.

Your phone does the footwork like this:

Call Forwarding lets you route your calls to <u>any</u> phone so you don't have to miss a call.

Call Forward—No Answer lets calls reach you at a pre-designated number when you can't easily get to your phone.

Call Forward—Busy automatically forwards your calls when you're already on your phone.

Get messages even while you're on the run—with our Call Answering service.

Here's an affordable and easy-to-use service that turns your phone into a message center. It uses a recording of your voice to receive and store messages.

When you're ready, just retrieve all those messages from your friends and business associates.

Don't miss a call. Get Call Forwarding and Call Answering and you're completely covered.

Stop playing telephone tag. To order these or any Custom Calling Features, or for more information, call ***777-1200*** (RESIDENCE) or ***777-1234*** (BUSINESS).

RochesterTelephone

For the way you live your life.

chapter TWO

Joe Herrera
Director of Marketing
Denny's Restaurants Inc.

Continuity is Crucial

Denny's Restaurants Inc. has been a part of everyday life for over 36 years. How is it that a company can continue to grow and prosper year after year?

Denny's is a family restaurant that appeals to people of all ages. Our product is food, but our business is to provide a complete dining experience: good food, friendly and efficient service, and an environment that makes our customers want to come back time and time again. Everyone in business knows that it is far easier to get a current customer back than it is to find, convince, and win over a new customer. So, once customers sample the Denny's dining experience, we want to keep them coming back.

That's continuity. It is crucial to our business and that's why we put so much effort into it.

The Flintstones family program was developed with just this objective in mind. We wanted to appeal to families, to make the dining experience memorable, positive, and fun for the kids so they would keep coming back. The program is not a one shot deal, but a fully integrated, year-long marketing, continuity program that remained fresh, new, and fun for our customers every time they came back to Denny's.

The program gained awareness and trial from the family customer base, but most importantly, it gave them a reason to come back! It's through continuity that businesses survive over the long haul. Denny's is proud that its Flintstone family program has been selected for this important chapter in this important book.

Direct Response Builds Circulation

CLIENT:

The Boston Globe

(Mary Jane Patrone)

AGENCY:

Berenson, Isham & Partners Inc.

(Paul Berenson)

When the *Boston Globe* wanted to extend its circulation in fringe areas, it turned to Berenson, Isham to work out a campaign using direct mail. The three areas the newspaper had in mind were Cape Cod, New Hampshire, and Worcester County, Massachusetts. Each of these has a strong local daily newspaper.

Cape Cod was the first area to be promoted, and the campaign was scheduled for the beginning of the summer vacation period. Homeowners in those communities where the *Globe* had home delivery service were sent a double postcard self-mailer, whose headline was "The Hottest Deal on the Cape this Summer," and it offered home delivery of the Sunday edition for 13 weeks at only 68¢ a week. The reply half of the card already had the homeowner's name and address on it, so all the new subscriber had to do was to check a box, tear it off, and drop it in the mail. Postage would be paid by the *Globe*. This postcard, which went by first class mail, was actually less expensive— 15¢ versus 16.7¢—than the slower third class bulk mail.

People who subscribed to the Sunday paper only were offered issues on the other six days of the week for only 97¢ a week, compared with the newsstand price of $1.50. An 8½ x 11, two-fold mailer was used, but with an unusual design which turned out to be an economy. The offer was "less than a buck," and the face of the mailing piece looked like a dollar with one corner missing. The addressee's name and address was attached to the tear-off segment that was an order form, and the die-cut permitted the same label to serve as the out-going address. This was also a prepaid business-reply card.

The headline on the second mailing read "The Best Deal in the Granite State This Fall," and in a format like the one used for the Cape Cod campaign, it offered the Sunday edition for the same 68¢ a week, but this time for 26 weeks. The copy emphasized the special New Hampshire section that was included each week with the regular *Boston Sunday Globe.*

For the third mailing, to Worcester County about 40 miles west of Boston, the format was maintained, but the headline was changed to "Rake in Big Savings This Fall," and the offer was the *Globe*, seven issues a week, for $1.75 a week. Since the *Globe*'s delivery area did not cover all of Worcester County, a super-imposed streamer that read "Exclusive Offer for Residents in Your Area Only" was part of the design.

The fourth mailing went out to residents in some of the suburban communities just south of Boston, to launch a new regional, *South Weekly.* The primary vehicle for the launch used the same double-postcard format that had proved successful in the earlier mailings, but a different format was sent out to a sample of 25 percent of the mailing list, as a test. It consisted of a window envelope containing a flyer and a business reply card, but this didn't do nearly as well as the double postcard.

Looking back at all variations of the mailing, the new, double postcard format outdid all previous promotions to the same areas. The New Hampshire and Worcester promotions doubled the previous results for those areas, while the Cape Cod promotion produced six times as many responses as an earlier mailing to that area.

Get The Globe delivered weekdays for less than a buck.

You already enjoy The Globe on Sundays. Now you can enjoy the rest of the week for an additional 97¢.

As a Boston Sunday Globe subscriber, we're making you this special offer. Sign up now for the daily Globe at 97¢, and we'll extend your Sunday subscription at the special 68¢ per week rate. That's right, you can enjoy The Globe *seven days* a week for an incredible *$1.65 per week.*

Then you can know what's happening from Barnstable to Bangkok, while enjoying an infinite variety of features, articles, and special daily sections. And remember only The Boston Globe can bring you this quality of reporting day in and day out.

Make your week complete. Sign up for 13 weeks of home delivery of the daily and Sunday Boston Globe. And save $14.30. Mail the enclosed card today or call toll-free 1-800-532-9524, ext. 50.

NO POSTAGE
NECESSARY
IF MAILED
IN THE
UNITED STATES

BUSINESS REPLY MAIL
FIRST CLASS   PERMIT NO. 20709   BOSTON, MA
Postage will be paid by addressee

The Boston Globe
Home Delivery Department
Boston, MA 02107

Cape Cod residents who already were Sunday subscribers were approached to extend their subscriptions.

The first mailing offered Cape Cod residents a special price for the Sunday paper.

☐ **YES,** Sign me up for 13 weeks of the Boston Sunday Globe at 68¢ a week (a total of only $8.84).

Home Phone: (_____)_____
Please check your name and address for accuracy.
Offer good for new subscribers only.

Berenson, Isham & Partners
Paul Berenson
9 Arch Street
Boston, MA 02101

Delivery will begin within 2–3 weeks from receipt of order.
Offer expires August 31, 1988.

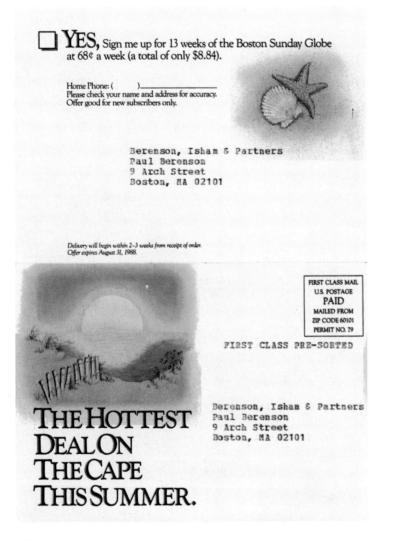

FIRST CLASS MAIL
U.S. POSTAGE
PAID
MAILED FROM
ZIP CODE 60101
PERMIT NO. 79

FIRST CLASS PRE-SORTED

Berenson, Isham & Partners
Paul Berenson
9 Arch Street
Boston, MA 02101

THE HOTTEST DEAL ON THE CAPE THIS SUMMER.

GET THE BOSTON SUNDAY GLOBE DELIVERED FOR ONLY 68¢.

Sign up for 13 weeks of the Boston Sunday Globe, and we'll deliver it to your doorstep for only 68¢ a week. But that's only half the story. Every week the Sunday Globe is packed with outstanding coverage of local, state, national and international news, sports, business, and the arts; features and commentary by Pulitzer-Prize winning writers; Parade Magazine, The Boston Globe Magazine, and America's most popular comic strips. And it's all yours for a cool 68¢ a week.

Brighten your Sundays with the hottest newspaper in New England. Start your 13-week home delivery of the Boston Sunday Globe today. Mail the attached card or call toll-free: 1-800-532-9524, ext. 50.

NO POSTAGE
NECESSARY
IF MAILED
IN THE
UNITED STATES

BUSINESS REPLY MAIL
FIRST CLASS   PERMIT NO. 20709   BOSTON, MA
Postage will be paid by addressee

The Boston Globe
Home Delivery Department
Boston, MA 02107

The first Cape Cod mailing was repeated for Southern New Hampshire, but this was for a 26-week period.

GET THE BOSTON SUNDAY GLOBE DELIVERED FOR ONLY 68¢.

Here's a deal from The Boston Globe that's as solid as a rock. Sign up for 26 weeks of the Boston Sunday Globe and we'll deliver it to your doorstep for only 68¢ a week. But that's only part of the story. Every week the Sunday Globe brings you local, state, national and international news, sports, business and the arts; features and commentary by Pulitzer Prize winning writers; Parade Magazine; The Boston Globe Magazine, America's most popular comic strips and a special New Hampshire Weekly section packed with local and state news and information.

And it's all yours for only 68¢ a week. To rake in big savings this fall on the Sunday Globe, start your subscription today. Mail the attached card or call toll-free: 1-800-225-9962, ext. 45.

||||

NO POSTAGE
NECESSARY
IF MAILED
IN THE
UNITED STATES

BUSINESS REPLY MAIL
FIRST CLASS   PERMIT NO. 20709   BOSTON, MA

Postage will be paid by addressee

The Boston Globe
Home Delivery Department
Boston, MA 02107

☐ **YES,** Sign me up for 26 weeks of the Boston Sunday Globe at 68¢ a week.

Home Phone: (_____) _____
Please check your name and address for accuracy.
Offer good for new subscribers only.

Horizon Direct Mail, Inc.
P. O. Box: 632
Hampton, NH 03842   XX

Delivery will begin 2-3 weeks from receipt of order.
Offer expires *December 31, 1988.*

FIRST CLASS MAIL
U.S. POSTAGE
PAID
MAILED FROM
ZIP CODE 60101
PERMIT NO. 79

FIRST CLASS PRE-SORTED

Horizon Direct Mail, Inc.
P. O. Box: 632
Hampton, NH 03842

THE BEST DEAL IN THE GRANITE STATE THIS FALL.

GET THE BOSTON GLOBE DELIVERED EVERYDAY FOR ONLY $1.75 A WEEK.

Here's a deal from The Boston Globe that's only available to residents in your area. Sign up for 26 weeks of The Boston Globe and we'll deliver it to your doorstep everyday for only $1.75 a week. But that's only part of the story. Every week The Globe brings you local, state, national and international news, sports, business and the arts; features and commentary by Pulitzer Prize-winning writers; Business Extra and Calendar Magazine so you can plan your weekend. And on Sunday you get The Boston Globe Magazine, Parade Magazine and America's most popular comic strips. It's all yours for only $1.75 a week. That's a substantial savings over the newsstand price. So rake in big savings this fall on The Globe, start your subscription today. Mail the attached card or call toll-free: 1-800-532-9524, ext. 25.

NO POSTAGE
NECESSARY
IF MAILED
IN THE
UNITED STATES

BUSINESS REPLY MAIL
FIRST CLASS   PERMIT NO. 20709   BOSTON, MA

Postage will be paid by addressee

The Boston Globe
Home Delivery Department
Boston, MA 02107

For Worcester County, the format was changed only slightly.

☐ **YES,** Sign me up for 26 weeks of The Boston Globe at $1.75 a week.

Home Phone: (_____)_____
Please check your name and address for accuracy.
Offer good for new subscribers only.

Berenson, Isham & Partners   XX
Andy Graff
31 Milk St
Boston MA 02109-5400

Delivery will begin 2–3 weeks from receipt of order.
Offer expires January 31, 1989.

EXCLUSIVE OFFER
FOR RESIDENTS IN
YOUR AREA ONLY.

FIRST CLASS MAIL
U.S. POSTAGE
PAID
MAILED FROM
ZIP CODE 60101
PERMIT NO. 79

FIRST CLASS PRE-SORTED

Berenson, Isham & Partners
Andy Graff
31 Milk St
Boston MA 02109-5400

RAKE IN BIG SAVINGS THIS FALL.

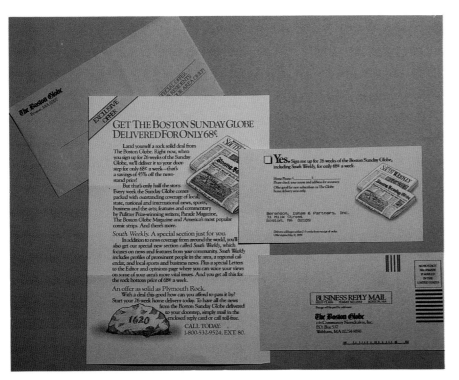

GET THE BOSTON SUNDAY GLOBE DELIVERED FOR ONLY 68¢.

EXCLUSIVE OFFER FOR RESIDENTS OF YOUR AREA ONLY.

Sign up for 26 weeks of the Boston Sunday Globe, and we'll deliver it to your doorstep for 68¢ a week. But that's only half the story. Every week the Sunday Globe comes packed with outstanding coverage of local, state, national and international news, sports, business and the arts; features and commentary by Pulitzer Prize-winning writers; Parade Magazine, The Boston Globe Magazine and America's most popular comic strips.

South Weekly. A special section just for you.

In addition to great news coverage from around the world, our new *South Weekly* section will give you news and features from around your community. *South Weekly* includes local sports and business news, people profiles and an opinions page where you can voice your views on some of your area's more vital issues. And it's all yours for only 68¢ a week.

Sign up now and you could be reading the Sunday Globe all summer long for only 68¢. To start your 26-week home delivery, simply mail the enclosed reply card or call toll-free today.

CALL TODAY:
1-800-532-9524, EXT. 65.

NO POSTAGE
NECESSARY
IF MAILED
IN THE
UNITED STATES

BUSINESS REPLY MAIL
FIRST CLASS   PERMIT NO. 05964   BOSTON, MA

Postage will be paid by addressee

The Boston Globe
c/o Community Newsdealers, Inc.
P.O. Box 537
Waltham, MA 02254-9890

☐ **Yes.** Sign me up for 26 weeks of the Boston Sunday Globe, including *South Weekly,* for only 68¢ a week.

Home Phone: (_____)
Please check your name and address for accuracy.
Offer good for new subscribers in The Globe home delivery area only.

SE2A

Berenson, Isham & Partners Inc
31 Milk Street
Boston, MA   02109

Delivery will begin within 2–3 weeks from receipt of order.
Offer expires May 31, 1989.

FIRST CLASS MAIL
U.S. POSTAGE
PAID
MAILED FROM
ZIP CODE 48068
PERMIT NO. 467

HERE'S THE OFFER YOU'VE BEEN WAITING FOR.

PRESORTED FIRST CLASS

Berenson, Isham & Partners Inc
OR CURRENT RESIDENT
31 Milk Street
Boston, MA   02109

Colorful Product— Colorful Promotion

CLIENT:
Kodak Canada Inc.

AGENCY:
Boulevard Strategic Marketing & Design, Toronto

AWARDS:
1989 CSPA Award of Excellence (Finalist)
1989 Bronze Spire Award (American Marketing Association)

Just because your name is well known and fully accepted doesn't mean that everything you offer the public is automatically accepted. Such was true of Kodak Canada. Although consumers bought Kodak products, the marketing thrust fell short of convincing them to start on Kodak film, use Kodak processing, and finish on Kodak photographic paper via the Colorwatch system. The company was receiving stiff competition, especially from strong, vertically-integrated retail chains, which represent a substantial share of consumer sales.

Historically, Kodak had marketed and promoted each of its three product lines separately, using two to six promotions each year, running at about the same time, but each independently, with separate themes and creative elements. In addition, it had initiated a regional promotional structure which further fractionated the total image, leading to a lack of cohesion and the danger of erosion of valuable brand identity.

Looking at the situation, the agency and Kodak worked together to develop a broad umbrella promotion that could be used nationally, could cover all three segments of the product line, and could be customized to meet the needs of major accounts, without diminishing the overall impact.

At first, Kodak had some doubts about the program. In the first place, it had never executed a multi-brand promotion. In addition, it had serious doubts about vesting all its promotional funds into a single program which would run for the entire year. But after considering the proposal in detail, it decided to go ahead with it, and gave the agency full authority to proceed.

The objectives of the promotion were stated very clearly in its outline. It was designed to stimulate multiple purchases of all Kodak consumer products by the consumer, to ensure purchases, and to generate enhanced brand awareness. This was to be achieved by saving evidence of purchases of Kodak products, and redeeming them for brilliantly-colored stuffed animals, dubbed Kodak Kolorkins Fantasy Creatures.

The sales force, of course, had to be motivated to produce strong sell-in efforts, and to get full merchandising support at store level, and the values of the promotion had to be sold to the trade to make sure that the offer was made clearly and prominently to the public.

The Fantasy Creatures fascinated the public. Their bright colors were cheerful (and incidentally reminded people of the bright colors of Kodak films), and the little animals had a lovable personality that attracted children of all ages, from babies to grandparents. It was indeed a family premium for a family product.

Once the Kolorkins, who were given immediately recognizable and special names like Kwikki, Kazoom, Kosmic, Klakki, Kitzi, Kabboo and Kizmo, were designed and produced, the concept was quickly and easily extended to other premiums such as tumblers, coloring books, growth charts, magnets, and pins. Some of these were used as giveaways, others as optional premiums to be obtained in exchange for product points.

The creatures were first introduced in a two-page free standing insert (FSI), and they made an appearance on counter cards and header cards.

They were tied into multi-pack offers which carried additional bonus points, and they even began to make personal appearances at such events as the Calgary Stampede, and the Winter Olympics. The idea has also attracted the attention of other Kodak companies around the world, including both Kodak US and Kodak Switzerland, with Kodak affiliates in both Spain and Australia endorsing the promotion.

In Canada, the results proved to be exciting. In 1988, redemptions of the toys exceeded projections by more than 150 percent!

The heroes of the promotion were the seven brightly-colored, fanciful stuffed animals, called the Kolorkins.

The promotion was announced to the public in a free-standing insert.

A special carton, in which the toys were shipped to the consumer, carried the warning, "This box contains living color."

Special promotional materials supported efforts developed by major outlets that wanted exclusive offers.

A special effort was made to promote Kolorkin-related items as holiday gifts.

FREE

In-Store Offer
Kodak Kolorkins Sweatshirt*
(sug. retail $29.95) or

Set of 4 Kodak Kolorkins Pins**
(sug. retail $8.95)

With the purchase of specified Kodak 35mm
Cameras and 3 rolls of Kodak colour film

Ask Us for Details!

PLUS
Send for a No-Charge
(postage, handling and taxes extra)
Kodak Kolorkins
fantasy creature

*With purchase of Kodak Model S500AF, S900 Tele, K80, K12, or K14 camera.
**With purchase of Kodak Model S100EF, S300MD, or K60 camera.

Sweatshirt design subject to change.

A variety of counter cards and other displays were developed for film sales, for photofinishing, and even for the Christmas holiday.

Point-of-purchase was available with specific individualization for special outlets.

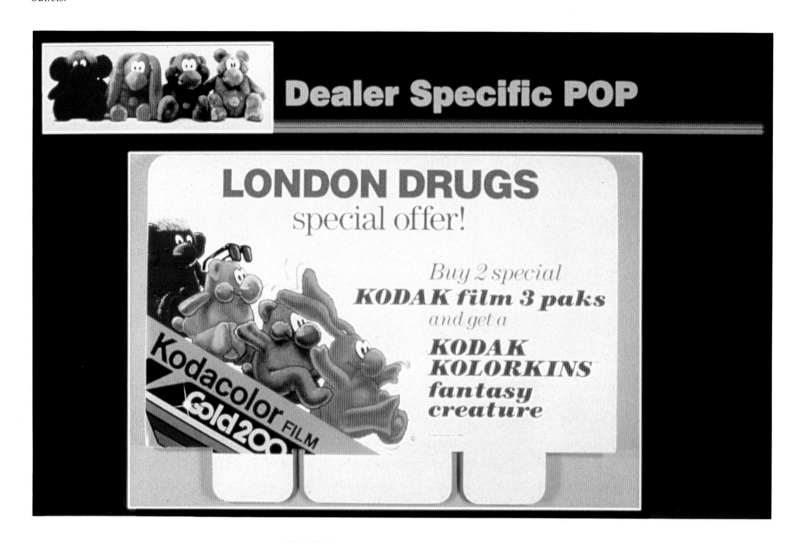

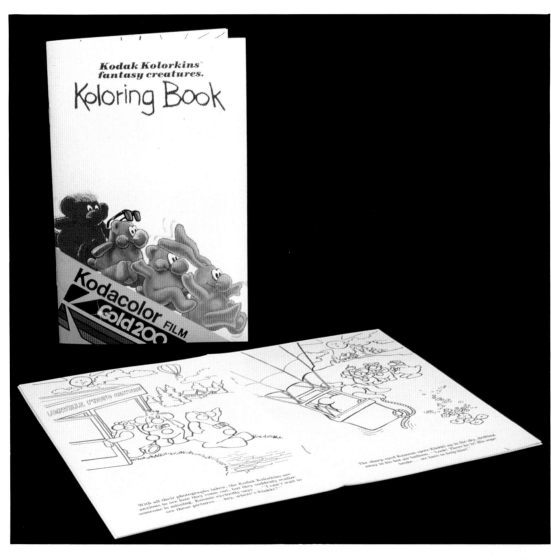

The characters were easy to use as the design element in special gift items, and a wide variety was developed and offered to consumers, in a myriad of ways.

Reaching Baseball Fans Where They Live

CLIENT:
Pepsi-Cola Company, Somers, NY

AGENCY:
Impact, Chicago
(Joseph P. Flanagan)

AWARDS:
1989 CSPA Award of Excellence
(Finalist)

Regional promotions have always been difficult to produce, since a limited area is difficult to create interest, and causes promotional materials either to suffer in comparison with materials created for national use, or become inordinately expensive. Here is an example of a regional campaign that had many of the benefits of a national one.

Baseball themes have always been attractive, especially for popular beverages, both beer and soft drinks, whose active users tend to be young and male. The problem has always been to tap into the enthusiasm of fans for their local teams, without adding to the campaign cost.

In this promotion, the sponsors were the Pepsi-Cola bottlers located in Wisconsin, Minnesota, North and South Dakota. They wanted to do a market-wide program that would utilize production efficiencies, through its canning cooperative known as WisPak. It would not stand alone, since Pepsi was about to have a national program with the theme "America's Hometown Choice," a follow-up on its successful taste test challenge.

The new promotion called for a system-wide under the cap/in the can program (known in the trade as UTC), which would run in every WisPak-supplied market. Designed to run the entire summer from April 1 through Labor Day, it would be a departure from the customary period of about 12 weeks for earlier UTC promotions. In addition, it had to be relevant to each of the separate markets within the four participating states, and be consistent with the America's Hometown Choice promotion.

To meet these criteria, the program developed a baseball theme, tying in with the appropriate major league baseball teams. In Wisconsin, the tie-in was with the Milwaukee Brewers, and with the Minnesota Twins in the other three states. It didn't hurt that the Twins had won the World Series in 1987, and that this promotion was scheduled for the summer of 1988, when memories were fresh and enthusiasm high.

The program was called "Count the Wins," and provided consumers two ways to win: continuity and instant, based on a number between 0 and 99 that was printed inside the can or on the cap. The major prize, a chance at $10,000, was offered to those purchasers whose numbers matched the number of winning games achieved by the local team on June 15. There was a second chance for games won by September 5.

But to keep a UTC program active, there must also be instant winners, and so the program included thousands of instant win prizes, including pairs of tickets to major league home games, 2-liter bottle or Pepsi, and $1,000 in cash.

Support was, of course, important. A variety of in-store promotional items, ranging from a header for an end aisle display to a shelf talker, from drop-in ads to TV spots utilizing a local baseball player, were made available to the bottlers and to the retailers.

Results went beyond what was originally expected. All key retailers cooperated by using incremental product display and feature ad support. What was especially gratifying was that consumer response was stronger than expected. Having two major winner dates kept the program active over the entire five-month period. Almost twice as many customers redeemed qualifying caps/cans for the September 5 drawing as for the June 15, suggesting that the program excitement continued to buld over the summer. While 140,000 qualifying numbers were turned in for the two territories on June 15, that number grew to 250,000 for the drawing on September 15.

Bottlers in St. Louis and Cincinnati offered the program the same summer in their territories, achieving similar strong sales and consumer response to the program. In Chicago, the bottler had been running his own very successful program, based on the number of home runs achieved by the Cubs, and was unwilling to risk his equity in his own promotion, but he saw the advantages of going along with the other bottlers in the joint production of promotional materials, even though the Chicago effort required slightly more personalization than in other markets. But the results— increased participation by consumers—paralleled those in other markets.

One of the most successful aspects of the program was Impact's ability to establish a format and standard for all elements of the program. This offered the opportunity to maximize efficiencies for the development and production of all point-of-sale elements. For the production of the television spots, for example, a single set was built and players were cycled through it during a two-day period. This resulted in a per market cost of $30,000 for the 30-second commercial, including the talent.

These countercards carried the message at the point of sale. Effectively the only difference is that one is identified with the Minnesota Twins, while the other with the Milwaukee Brewers.

When the promotion reached St.
Louis, there was a change of design
in the central panel and, of course,
the appearance of the cardinal of
the baseball team.

The Chicago header was also a
countdown, but it added instant
prizes that tied in with Burger King.

Catalog Production under Control

CLIENT:
Lumbermans Merchandising
Corp., Wayne, PA
(Jack Scharff)

AGENCY:
Metro Seliger Industries,
Woodside, NY
(Richard Skolnik, Harold Hershbain, Art
Nechamkin, Julius Golden)

Getting out more than 50 different catalogs, each adapted to a different retailer, with a different selection of merchandise and different prices, can be a very complex situation, and one which is prone to mistakes. But MSI has been doing it now for 25 years, working with the member stores of the Lumbermens Merchandising Corp.

In order to accomplish this requires a successful system. One must remember that the member/dealers of LMC are all independent, each with its own merchandise mix, partially dependent on the part of the country in which it is located, but also upon the nature of each store's clientele. Although the catalogs are similar in format and design, the contents vary greatly, as do prices and store "images." In addition, dealers are offered a choice of three cover designs and three sizes. Catalogs are produced in a 32-page edition, 8½" x 11"; a 64-page edition 5³/₈" x 8½"; and a 32-page mini, 5³/₈" x 8½".

The catalogs are released in April of each year, but the process starts in the fall of the preceding year, when promotion to the dealer organization starts. Prototype catalogs are distributed at the LMC annual meeting in November, at which time most of the catalog orders are received from dealers. This tells MSI how many catalogs, and which types, will be needed, but not their content.

Assembly kits are sent to all who have decided to participate. The dealer indicates the product units, both art and copy, he wants to include. He can select items from his previous catalog, or from those put together for other dealers, or specify new merchandise. He may also select his items by checking off the product he wants to include on a computer printout of available merchandise.

The dealers' paste-ups are returned to MSI in January and February, and the MSI art and production departments get the material prepared for the printer. Because of fluctuating lumber prices, MSI telephones each participating dealer for last-minute price changes just before the catalogs go to press.

In recent years, an optional 16-page section giving how-to tips and detailed project directions has been offered to dealers, resulting in increased retention by homeowners.

A kit of promotional materials, which includes newspaper ads, radio scripts, news releases, and in-store signs, is sent to the dealers to help them give the catalog optimum advertising support.

Guide To A Beautiful Home

J.E. SMITH

The Lumber People Since 1897

621 BANK STREET, WATERBURY
756-8051

Not responsible for typographical errors. Prices are liable to change with or without notice. Prices good from March 16, 1989 through May 31, 1989.

Each catalog is identified with the names and addresses of the stores which have ordered them. The contents of each catalog is chosen from a large selection of artwork.

This mailing included testimonials from happy users, and offered a personal consultation to develop a catalog, especially for new users.

Dear Jack,

I accept your offer of one-to-one presentation of the 1990 catalog at my yard. Please call me to make the necessary arrangements.

Name _____

Company _____

Tel. ( ) _____

SPEAKING OF CATALOGS...

What dealers say about the 1989 LMC catalog

> "Customers like it. People look forward to receiving it and hold on to it. We look at the catalog as a long-term sales aid more than just a quickie sale."
> Dykes Lumber Co., Inc.
> Weehawken, NJ

> "Store traffic picked up immediately. The catalog is very good for us...works well year after year. It's a great promotion...customers use it for a long time and look forward to it coming out."
> Curtis Lumber Co., Inc.
> Ballston Spa, NY

> "As usual, things went crazy again when our catalog came out. Traffic increased a lot, and the phone was ringing off the hook. Most of that is still going on weeks later, because the catalog is really a year-round selling tool with us, not a sale promotion. We expect action from the catalog, and we're not disappointed."
> Ring's End, Inc.
> Darien, CT

> "All seven of our stores reported a good increase, and many of them indicated that the catalog was a better traffic-producer than any circular. Our special catalog pricing and sale dates brought in customers that bought. Contractors, too, are holding on to the catalog and are using it with their customers."
> Conklin and Strong, Inc.
> Warwick, NY

A kit sent to catalog users included slicks that could be used in local newspaper ads, and sample press releases and radio spot copy.

HOW TO USE THIS KIT

ADS

1. Use the "teaser" ads to build up excitement before your catalog sale event actually begins. Have your newspaper insert a different product each time the ad runs. You can run these ads throughout your catalog event.

2. Run the small, medium and large size ads throughout your catalog event, inserting any catalog merchandise you wish to promote.

PRICE SIGNS

1. Place them on catalog merchandise throughout your store and yard, with the price of each item clearly marked in the blank space.

2. The larger size price signs have enough space for you to write product descriptions or any other message you wish, such as "No More When These Are Gone," "We Bought Big to Save You More," etc.

3. If you require more price signs, give us a call.

WINDOW AND IN-STORE SIGNS

1. Use these signs in windows, on walls and throughout your store and yard.

2. More signs are available if you need them.

LABELS FOR CATALOG COVERS

Use these "PRICES HAVE CHANGED" labels to affix to the catalogs you have left over and wish to distribute after your catalog sale event.

TAKE ONE CONTAINERS

Use them to hold copies of your catalog on counters or near cash registers.

RADIO COMMERCIALS

1. Run the 30-second spot and the 60-second spots as often as possible during your catalog event.

2. Be sure to fill in all blank spaces before giving the spots to your radio station.

NEWS RELEASE

1. Submit it to your local newspaper with your name and company name inserted wherever indicated.

2. If you wish, our catalog agency will submit it to your local paper. Send it to Metro Seliger Industries (MSI) with the name of the paper you wish it to appear in. We cannot promise, of course, that the paper will run it exactly as submitted.

LMC CATALOG MERCHANDISING KIT   <u>Spring 1989</u>

<u>NEWS RELEASE</u>

FREE HOW-TO-BUILD-IT BOOKLET COMES WITH
FREE CATALOG FROM LOCAL HOME CENTER

When homeowners in the (name of city) area found the big new 1989 catalog from (Dealer Name) in their mail boxes, they got much more than they bargained for. First of all, they received a colorful, comprehensive catalog of home improvement products, building materials and do-it-yourself needs at very attractive prices. Everything that (Dealer Name) stocks is represented in the new publication - lumber, plywood, ceilings, floors, roofing, siding, wall paneling, doors, windows, tools, hardware and much, much more. And the prices during (Dealer Name's) Catalog Sale Days are almost irresistible.

Plus...there was a valuable bonus in the catalogs that (Dealer Name's) customers and prospective customers received - a bound-in multi-page booklet of instructions for building eleven useful and attractive objects to enhance home and property. The handsome how-to-build-it booklet, called "Do-It-Yourself Dream Projects," contains easy-to-follow instructions and lists of materials for constructing a deck and accessories, storage units, a dog house, a mail box stand, a workbench and more.

"To make it even easier for our customers, says _____ of (Dealer Name), "we calculated the total cost of materials for many of these projects, and printed those prices elsewhere in our catalog. Since many shoppers brings their catalogs right into our yard and store to use as a shopping guide, we expect that quite a few will be picking up the materials for some of these D-I-Y projects while they're here. They'll probably have questions about them,too, and our salespeople are all expert enough to give them authoritative answers."

But surely not everyone in the area has received a catalog? "No, but thousands have," says Mr. _____. "Anyone who hasn't is invited to come in and pick up a free copy, including the how-to-build-it section. We're proud of our catalog, and we're glad that our customers find it so helpful.

(Dealer Name's) main yard is located at _____. The firm also has yards in _____, _____ and _____.

LMC CATALOG MERCHANDISING KIT   <u>Spring 1989</u>

60-SECOND RADIO COMMERCIAL

ANNOUNCER:

The sale that every homeowner in the (name of city) area has been waiting for has arrived...and you can get a pretty good idea of what it's all about just be sitting in your easy chair and browsing through the new catalog from (Dealer Name). Haven't received your free copy? Better hurry in to (Dealer Name) and pick one up during Catalog Sale Days. While you're there, take a good look at the price tags on building materials, do-it-yourself products, tools and hardware. You'll hardly believe your eyes! For example, _____, regularly $_____, are only $_____; _____ have been reduced by more than _____%; _____, usually $_____, are now two for $_____; _____ are priced a full $_____ below (Dealer Name's) everyday low price. Big as it is, (Dealer Name's) catalog shows only a representative selection of what savings are in store for you...so put your home improvement dreams together and come on over to (Dealer Name's) Catalog Sale. It's on now, but it won't be on for long. (Dealer Name and Address).

This Promotion Offered New Records

CLIENT:
Johnnie Walker Red Label,
Schieffelin & Somerset Co.,
New York

AGENCY:
Focus Marketing Inc.,
Norwalk, CT
(Bernie Trueblood, Charles Roth,
Eve Gilbert)

The slogan on top of the stack header read, "He has a great collection...And he drinks Johnnie Walker." Representative of the brand's current advertising, this slogan not only reminded drinkers of Scotch of the image of Walker Red, but it also introduced a way that buyers of the product could build up their own great collection.

The mechanism was simple. Every purchase of Johnnie Walker Red Label was worth $4 toward the purchase of a CD, record, or cassette tape. The customer picked up a catalog of selected tapes/CDs, wrote his selections on the order blank, attached any number of the bar codes from the back of the bottle, and sent in his order.

The selected catalogs were available at the point-of-purchase display, or in a shelf-talker. Although the catalogs listed only 355 selections, over 35,000 were listed in the full catalog available from Express Music, which handled the fulfillment for Walker. They included music to suit every taste, from Classical and Musical Theater through Popular and Rock and Roll.

The offer was advertised in national publications, but the bulk of the promotion was handled through displays at stores that sold liquor. Catalogs, which included order blanks, were available from pockets mounted on the headers. Similar pockets were designed so that store management could use them as shelf-talkers or as tents at the check-out counter.

One of the neat things about this promotion was that it required a minimum effort on the part of the importer or the store. There were no coupons to be collected at the retail level, no handling of individual mail at Walker. The orders and labels went directly to the distributor, who shipped the tapes and/or CDs directly back to the purchaser.

This ease of participation contributed to a large increase in display activity during the promotion period, and in an unusual result for the spirits business; the promotion was scheduled for an annual re-run.

The counter card, like the shelf-talker, had a pocket for take-one folders.

The shelf-talker shipped flat, and had an adhesive strip already applied for mounting. It could also stand by itself on a counter.

The complete catalog of the distributor, which was available to all participants, held over 35,000 titles.

Profits Will Soar To The Top Of Your Charts
<u>And</u> It's All From Johnnie Walker Red®

Johnnie Walker
RED LABEL

The simple promotion card showed both the case card and the shelf-talker that was offered.

Top Your Profit Charts With This Hit Promotion

Sing to the tune of success with a Johnnie Walker Red promotion that's a sure-fire hit.

* **Your shoppers save $4.00** on CD's and Tapes every time they buy Johnnie Walker Red Label.*

* They can order an Express Music catalog, offering over 35,000 titles and $50.00 of coupons!

There are two things shoppers just can't get enough of . . . Johnnie Walker Red Label . . . and Music. And you can give it all to them.

Everything you need to encourage continous sales is provided in this super promotion:

"He has a great collection And he drinks Johnnie Walker."

FREE CDs & TAPES
WITH PROOFS OF PURCHASE

Johnnie Walker **RED LABEL**

CASE CARD 16" x 22"
This eye-catching display captures the attention of your customers, reflecting Johnnie Walker's bold graphic design. It features take-one brochures and enhances Johnnie Walker's trend-setting advertising.
Code #: H0056 (FREE), H0057 (CASH)
Packed: 10

TAKE-ONE BROCHURE
Consumers can order right away from this take-one featuring hundreds of music titles, FREE with purchases of Johnnie Walker Red.

SHELF TALKER / COUNTER UNIT 8" x 3½"
Holds consumer take-one and fits perfectly on your register, counter or shelf.
Code #: H0058
(Free version only)
Packed: 25

FREE CDs & TAPES   RED LABEL

Now You've Got It All!
So don't miss the beat! Tie-in now with this promotion and make Johnnie Walker your number one selling hit!

*Where legal. Alternative non-free offer available elsewhere.

Another 8½″x11″ card explained the offer to customers. It was printed on pressure sensitive stock so the dealer could mount it on any convenient surface.

OVER 35,000 CD's & TAPES

Johnnie Walker® RED LABEL

FREE

EXPRESS MUSIC CATALOG

WITH PROOFS OF PURCHASE

PICK YOUR LABEL FROM JOHNNIE WALKER RED

Welcome to the world's largest record store in paperback brought to you by Johnnie Walker Red, the World's Best Selling Scotch. Shop at your convenience – anytime, day or night. The Express Music Catalog puts every kind of music right at your fingertips.

HERE'S HOW IT WORKS

To order CD's or Tapes, make your selection from the Express Music Catalog. List the selections you want on one of the Express Music Order Forms located on the back of each Subscriber Discount Coupon. Total your purchases.

Collect the back label from any 750 ml., 1 litre or 1.75 litres bottle of Johnnie Walker Red and deduct $4.00 off the listed price for every Red back label you enclose. There's no limit to the number of labels you may enclose! No facsimiles will be honored.

Enter the amount deducted on the line on the order form entitled "Less Credit No." (see sample below)

Merchandise Subtotal	$ **40.00**
Less discount coupon on reverse	$ (**5.00**)
Sales Tax: NY State residents add 4¼%/NY City 8¼%	$ _____
Shipping, Handling and Insurance	$ 3.65
Less Credit (# proofs-of-purchase) $4.00 each proof	$ (**20.00**)
TOTAL	$ **18.65**

For example, if you have collected 5 labels, you can deduct $20.00 from your order. Each proof is worth $4.00; however, no credit or refunds can be given for any unused portion.

The $3.65 **per order** shipping, handling and insurance fee must be paid in the form of money order, check or credit card payment and cannot be paid with a Johnnie Walker Red Label.

As you're browsing through the over 35,000 titles listed in your catalog, keep these things in mind.

Express Music guarantees 100% satisfaction with every order – or you will be fully refunded. You'll receive only original manufacturer recordings. And if a requested selection is out of stock, Express Music will back order the recording or issue a credit certificate.

We're looking forward to hearing from you.

Offer expires December 31, 1989. Offer valid in U.S. Void where prohibited, taxed or restricted. Purchaser certifies that he/she is of legal drinking age under the laws of home state.

Johnnie Walker Red Label, Blended Scotch Whisky, 43.4% alc./vol. (86.8 Proof), © Schieffelin & Somerset Co., New York, NY

The take-one folder listed 355 albums, in both CD and cassette formats, that could be obtained at a discount. An order blank was also included.

A Luxury Life
for a Simple Act

CLIENT:
Telecom Canada Inc., Ottawa

AGENCY:
Gaylord Planned Promotions,
Rexdale, ON

Telecom Canada is the marketing arm for the ten telephone companies that provide residential service for the entire country. In 1988, it decided to execute the first national long distance contest involving all 10 provincial member telephone companies.

The concept was simple. All an entrant had to do was to make at least three long distance calls between April 1 and May 31, and send in an entry blank, giving the called numbers and when the calls were made. At the end of the contest, one entry would be selected, and the grand prize winner would be presented with a luxury Chrysler New Yorker, and enough cash to permit the winner to turn it in for a similar model every year of his life. This was to be done by issuing the winner an annuity indexed to inflation. Eleven additional draws awarded a single New Yorker to regional winners across the country.

Details of the sweepstakes and entry forms were included in a four-color folder inserted in the regular telephone bills of the millions of Bell residential subscribers. The direct mailer was sent twice, and was supported by print, radio, and television advertising. In addition, an eye-catching point-of-purchase display was set up in Bell's tele-boutique centers. This served as a supply of entry forms, and subscribers could also deposit their filled-in forms at the boutiques.

While actual figures are confidential, the pre-promotion targets were substantially exceeded. The sweepstakes generated the highest consumer entry level of any contest for the last ten years, and was approximately four times higher than forecast.

Talk yourself into a luxury

Enter the Telecom Canada National Long Distance Contest.

The four-color folder could fit into the regular billing envelopes. It held details of the sweepstakes, and an entry form.

car for life.

This floorstand, with its giant phone, was set up in the teleboutique centers run by the 10 regional companies. It held a supply of the entry forms, and a slot in the base of the phone was used to deposit filled-in forms.

Encouraging Things that Go Together

CLIENT:
Christie Brown & Co., Toronto

AGENCY:
Gaylord Planned Promotions,
Rexdale, ON

Although Oreo cookies are the number one brand in the Canadian cookie market, penetration was a mere 13 percent of Canadian households. Furthermore, studies indicated that for every purchase of Oreos, the consumer was making seven other cookie purchases. Christie was therefore faced with a group of customers who, while buying more Oreos than any other single brand, also purchased a significant number of other cookie brands.

Research also indicated that the brand's image was one of "wholesomeness," and that Oreos are usually eaten with milk or another beverage. Tying in to this relationship, Christie and its sales promotion agency decided to reward buyers of Oreos for regular purchase by giving them a coupon worth $2.50 toward the purchase of any size package of Oreos plus a one-liter size or larger container of milk. The consumer simply saved four Oreo proofs-of-purchase and sent them in for redemption, along with an official entry blank.

In-store promotional support was provided by one million flashed packages, info-center posters, header cards, shelf talkers, ad pads, and a 50¢ retailer in-ad coupon, good toward the joint purchase of milk and Oreos. With a total budget of $250,000, including the in-ad coupon, the promotion achieved a 36 percent increase in market share over the previous year. March/April shipments reached an all-time high. Participation rate was greater than double the norm for this type of promotion.

The same illustration, featuring a stack of Oreos and a pitcher of milk, was used on the refund coupon.

MILK 'N COOKIES SAVINGS – REQUEST FORM

To receive one store coupon worth $2.50 off the joint purchase of one litre (or larger) of milk plus one package of **OREO**® cookies (any size/variety) mail 4 UPC code symbols (the series of bars and numbers) from any 4 **OREO** cookie packs and your complete printed name and address to:

    MILK'N COOKIES OFFER
    P.O. BOX 9887
    SAINT JOHN, NEW BRUNSWICK
    E2L 4P3

Allow 4-6 weeks for delivery of your $2.50 coupon. Only requests providing 4 **OREO** cookie bar code symbols will qualify for this offer.

Mechanically reproduced proof-of-purchase symbols are not acceptable. Offer limited to one request per family, group or organization. Offer expires June 30, 1986.

® Registered Trade Mark of Nabisco Brands Ltd

1986. Sponsored by Christie Brown & Co., 2150 Lakeshore Blvd. West, Toronto, Ontario M8V 1A3. Offer good only in Canada. Void where not permitted by law.

NAME: _____

ADDRESS: _____ APT. _____

CITY: _____

PROVINCE: _____ POSTAL CODE: _____

PLEASE CHECK ONE BOX
Normally, how often do you buy **OREO** cookies?
Once every: ☐ 6 weeks ☐ 6 months ☐ Never
  ☐ 4 weeks ☐ 10 weeks ☐ 12 months Code a

109

The Mad Hatter Sells Tea

CLIENT:
Thomas J. Lipton, Toronto
(Jan Mollenhauer, Scott Greenwood)

AGENCY:
Promotions Solutions Group,
Toronto
(Leslee Vivian, Dermot O'Brien, Ian McLean)

A lot of tea is drunk in Canada, and the leading manufacturer of tea is Thomas J. Lipton, with a family of tea brands. Within the category, there is a tendency for consumers to stick with a group of 2 or 3 brands, buying the one that seems to offer the lowest price at the time they are in the market. Lipton itself has a number of different brands on the tea shelves. In addition, the name Lipton is associated more closely with soups than with tea, so there was a need to establish an image for the family of brands under a common theme.

The whole promotion was built around the Mad Hatter's Tea Party from the Lewis Carroll classic, *Alice in Wonderland*, with a sweepstakes as the major constituent. The grand prize was a ten-day trip for two, a mad trip, to visit the famous castles and sights of Alice's Wonderland of North Wales. The prize had an estimated value of $5,000.

But everybody could win, simply by sending in proofs of purchase from two of the Lipton brands of tea, and from one package of the store brand of cookies, along with an official entry blank. Including cookies in the deal not only made sense, for tea and cookies go together, but it shrewdly helped to sell the promotion to store management, since the house brand of cookies is a very profitable item.

The stores were drawn into the promotion by way of a local drawing, this for a limited edition Mad Hatter's Tea Pot, which was made exclusively for Lipton by Royal Stafford. The pot was incorporated into the sweepstakes display, carefully locked in position. A special ballot box on the display made it possible for the store manager to hold a drawing limited to his store, to select a winner of the tea pot, while other ballots were sent on for the grand prize drawing.

Die-cut stacker cards announced the sweepstakes and the free tea offer. Ad pads on the shelf and the display carried all the details of the promotion, as well as a sweepstakes entry form and the request for the free tea offer, which in itself was an automatic sweepstakes entry. The promotion was announced to the trade with a trade teaser, a sell-in brochure, and ads in the two grocery trade publications, *Canadian Grocer* and *L'Epicier.*

The promotion met or exceeded all objectives, prompting Lipton to follow-up with a similar promotion in 1989. Consumer coupons sent in were the largest number ever in a Lipton promotion: approximately 2,000. This was particularly impressive, since there was a high purchase requirement.

The colorful promotion material included die-cut cards in a variety of sizes. While minor changes were made from the first year to the second, they weren't obvious to the average consumer.

A separate entry blank was made available to the store manager if he wished to hold a drawing for the teapot on display. This did not remain as an element of the second year's promotion.

A MAD ● OFFER.
FREE TEA.
Buy any **2** participating brands of tea you're simply mad about, plus **1** package of store brand cookies. Mail in for free tea.

WIN A
MAD TRIP.
Visit the famous castles and sights of Alice's Wonderland of North Wales, Great Britain. One mad trip for two plus $1,000 in spending money to be won. Contest closes: July 31, 1988.

See all the simply mad details on reverse.
*TM Thomas J. Lipton Inc.

● FREE*
TEA TOWELS HOW MAD!

WIN A BRITISH CASTLE TOUR SIMPLY MAD!

Contest closes July 31, 1989.
*Send $1.50 to cover postage & handling.

See all the simply mad details on reverse. *®Thomas J. Lipton Inc.

TEA PARTY

Of course I'd like to win a Limited Edition Mad Hatter's Tea Pot by Royal Stafford. I'd be simply mad not to enter.

NAME _____

ADDRESS _____

CITY _____ PROV. _____

POSTAL CODE _____ TEL _____

*TM Thomas J. Lipton Inc.

Cartoon Characters Reach Kids

CLIENT:
Denny's Restaurants, Irvine, CA
(Joe Herrera)

AGENCY:
Strottman Marketing Inc.,
Irvine, CA
(Tom Wong)

AWARDS:
1989 CSPA Award of Excellence
(Best of Category)

Trying to reach children and their parents takes a promotion with depth and staying power. That's what Denny's Restaurants got when it asked Strottman Marketing to come up with a major, year-long promotional event.

The need to do something had become apparent; the family/mid-scale restaurant segment was suffering a downward trend. Although this kind of restaurant offered low prices with complete service, families with young children more often frequented fast food restaurants because of their perceived fun dining experience. Denny's wanted to build its customer base by attracting families with children under 10, and motivating them to become long-term, steady customers.

There were a number of factors that had to be taken into account when developing a program. First of these was the fact that Denny's had no program directed at the segment of families with kids, nor did their competitors in the segment. However, quick service restaurant chains had been successful in offering strong incentives to these very families. Fast food had established a deep-seated habit of visitation among these families, and Denny's realized that a short-term promotion would not be enough to change established behavior.

Early in the development of the promotion, it became clear that there were four key objectives:

- Achieve long-term penetration of families with kids under 10
- Increase guest counts in this segment
- Encourage repeat visits
- Improve overall sales and profitability without relying on food discounting.

The Flintstones seemed to be the perfect answer to reflect the Denny's dining experience. They represented a strong family image, and they would easily be recognized not only by kids, but also by baby boomers, young adults, parents, and seniors. They were solid, with 30 years of staying power, and they could be adapted to many aspects of dealing with children.

It started with a complete redesign of the children's menu, which added theme food items that would entice a child's imagination, as well as an appetite. Standard items on the menu were renamed, given such spectacular titles as Corndogasaurus, Brontosaurus Burger, Pterodactyl Egg Sandwich, and so on. Colorful characters and scenes on both sides of the menu made it fun for kids.

A series of activity books was designed to entertain kids while waiting for their food. Each book featured a Flintstone story along with games, puzzles, and jokes. A new book was released each month, which encouraged repeat visits to Denny's. Premiums, which were developed around the Flintstone characters, are a key to building family guest counts without discounting food prices. Four sets of premiums were designed, one for each quarter, with each set having three different designs in order to encourage frequent visits. The first set consisted of 8" plush characters—Fred, Dino, and Baby Puss. The second set was made up of reusable placemats. These had Flintstone scenes on one side, and games and activities on the other. A third set was a series of children's plates, of high quality plastic, each of which had a classic Flintstone scene.

A birthday club was a special promotion within a promotion. Children were urged to enter by filling out forms which were available at the restaurants or by mailing in a coupon in each of the activity books. Members were sent a custom Flintstone Birthday Card which invited the birthday child to come in for a free children's meal and a birthday sundae. It was a rare occurrence for a "Birthday Child" to come in for the free meal without several friends or family members.

The promotion was supported by a series of television commercials; Denny's first ever designed to reach kids. Each was built around one of the sets of premiums. Radio was used as a reminder to adults, once the promotion had been established by television. Newspaper ads were created for each premium, especially for use in smaller markets.

Such a program was a brand new experience for store managers and crew, and a special effort was developed to prepare the staff for the implementation of the project. The Manager's Kit included a program folder, advertising materials, crew buttons, and the first issue of a regular newsletter, called *Bedrock News*, which was released at intervals throughout the year. This kit brought awareness and excitement to each store before the program was implemented.

Trade support was nearly unanimous before the start of the program, and those few who hesitated got on the bandwagon as soon as early results began to get around. Customer traffic objectives were exceeded and guest counts were increased in all markets, as were net sales, party size, and average checks. And finally, profitability increases were in double digits during the period of the promotion.

Promotional materials included the three sets of premiums, each with its own countertop display, some of the books that were given away at each visit to the restaurant (left front), a special kids' menu (front center), and internal newsletters (right front) which kept restaurant staff excited about the promotion.

These countertop displays each held an actual sample of the premium. A third display was used for the stuffed characters.

A new fun book, designed to be given free to each visitor under 10, was released each month to help build continuity.

VOLUME 8

Denny's

Hanna-Barbera presents

THE FLINTSTONES FUN BOOK

- FUN COMICS
- PUZZLES GAMES

THIS BOOK BELONGS TO:

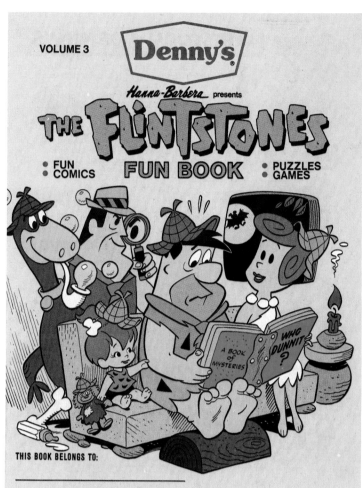

VOLUME 3

Denny's

Hanna-Barbera presents

THE FLINTSTONES FUN BOOK

- FUN COMICS
- PUZZLES GAMES

THIS BOOK BELONGS TO:

DRAW the EYES

EACH PAIR OF EYES SHOWN HERE FITS A SITUATION BELOW! DRAW IN THE EYES WHERE THEY BELONG!

1 2 3 4 5

Answers— A-3, B-2, C-4, D-1, E-5

BEDROCK WINDOW COUNT

EVERY BUILDING HAS THE SAME NUMBER OF WINDOWS ON THE OTHER SIDE. HOW MANY WINDOWS ARE THERE ALL TOGETHER? HOW MANY PALM TREES?

Answers— THERE ARE EIGHTY WINDOWS and EIGHT PALM TREES.

A colorful folder, with the Flintstone characters, was designed to hold the material that introduced the program to store managers and owners.

The Modern Stone-Age Lunch Box.

Only at Denny's.

Just in time for school.
The Flintstones Lunch Box.
Available in two colors
and two designs.
Take one home
to your cave kid.

Only
$**5**.^{99}
plus tax

While supplies last

89204

Table tents helped promote the sale of Flintstone premiums.

Everybody Likes Recipes

CLIENT:
Ultramar Canada Inc.,
St. John's NF
(Michele Coughlan)

AGENCY:
Target Marketing &
Communications Inc., St. John's,
NF, Canada
(Jackie Gale-Vaillancourt)

For 25 years, Ultramar Canada Ltd. has been an important part of the Newfoundland retail gasoline market, and, at least during the period of this promotion, was the leader in that province. In 1986, it bought the gulf network in eastern Canada, not only adding to its Newfoundland holdings, but making its first move into the Maritimes— Nova Scotia, New Brunswick and Prince Edward Island.

While Ultramar's corporate headquarters is in Quebec, it has been so strong in Newfoundland, that Newfoundlanders have thought of it as a native of the province, and even with its expansion into the other Maritimes, it has retained a strong regional tie. It is a valuable image, and one which management wished to retain.

However, the retail gasoline business is a highly competitive one, with an increasing trend toward brand switching and price consideration. Here regional brands are at a disadvantage since they must spread the cost of promotion over a smaller sales volume, and must therefore utilize creativity and ingenuity to match the impact of the more expensive programs produced by national brands.

That's what the "Traditional Recipes of Atlantic Canada" was all about. It pre-empted an area in which the national brands had no inherent advantage, and stressed the regional loyalties of the patrons and the company. The promotion used a series of 12 recipe books and a cooking guide, with a specially designed binder to hold all 13 books. One book was given away free with every purchase of 30 or more liters of gasoline.

The books used regional recipes that might not be found in most cookbooks, and yet were welcome and traditional. All the illustrations of finished dishes were in full color, and color photographs of typical regional scenes added to the attractiveness of the series.

The books were available during the three summer months of 1988, giving motorists enough opportunity to get the series, assuming an average fill-up of every ten days. This number was strategically chosen to entice consumers to complete their set. Another incentive was the offer of a binder, sold for $2.99 with no gasoline purchase required. The hope that once the binder was bought, there would be a further incentive to acquire the recipe books.

The promotion was supported by television advertising, which was able to portray the visual appeal of the books and the recipes. Radio was used to reach drivers in selective geographical markets, catching them at times when they would be likely to be looking for a gasoline station. Press releases obtained a very favorable response, with good coverage throughout the season, while television interviews and radio "trivia" contests helped spread the word.

Point-of-purchase, of course, was used heavily at the gas stations. Pole signs attracted people as they drove by the stations. Pump toppers provided more detail, especially about the binder, which had to be sold to the consumer. Flyers with details were used as pump handouts and inserted into monthly charge account statements. Local stations sometimes used them in special ways, like leaving leaflets under wipers of cars in nearby parking lots.

During the 1988 summer season, gasoline volume was 20 percent above that of the same period in 1986, and equalled the high achieved in 1987 through a promotion that was built around a very popular "Scenes of Atlantic Canada" series. Total gasoline sales in 1988 turned out to be about 10 percent greater than had been forecast, despite a summer of extremely poor weather and a subsequent decline in tourist activity. Of particular interest was the result of a random sample research held after the promotion. It indicated that of those who had collected the series, 15 percent said they were previously infrequent Ultramar users, but had since switched brands to become regulars.

A poster featured the binder, which was sold, in contrast to the recipe booklets which were given away free with a gasoline purchase.

There were 13 recipe booklets, each 6¹/₈''x8³/₈'', three-hole punched to fit in an attractive binder.

Each spread in the booklet showed a full-color picture of the dish whose ingredients and instructions were on the right.

own destinies. And they came ashore to a land which explorer Jacques Cartier called "...the fairest that it may be possible to see".

The earliest settlers were the French Acadians...a rugged, independent people who struggled to carve out a new life in the Island's wilderness...clearing dense forests, hauling massive stumps, cultivating and tilling the rich, red soil, and building homesteads with the 'rough logs they cut to build their huts'.

At the end of the Seven Years' War, their 'Isle St. Jean' was renamed to honour the heir to the British Throne. Then, after the American Revolution, a flood of United Empire Loyalists found refuge on the Island...followed by waves of Scottish, Irish and Lebanese immigrants during the 1800s. And the blending of these nationalities...together with their customs, traditions and cultures...is evident today in the easy smiles, strong work ethic, and tasty cuisine of Islanders from Cape Wolfe to Cape Bear.

Sample the rich harvest from the fertile red soil of this 'Garden of the Gulf'...and taste the unique blending of food traditions found in this and all twelve recipe books in this series.

A large banner was designed to mount on posts in the service station, to catch the passing driver's eye.

chapter THREE

Robert B. Konikow

Image—the Ubiquitous Goal

Our image is always with us, and everything we do affects it. This is true whether we are talking about an individual, a company, a product, or a service. Any time we present ourselves, we do something, perhaps good, perhaps bad, to our image.

And since the image people have of us is at the basis of how they react to us, to what we do and what we say, building the right image is important. Every case history included in this book has its effect on the company that sponsored the program.

Remember that most companies project an image that has been developed over the years. Customers and prospects look at a new promotion, get a feeling for the image it presents, and compares the image with their knowledge of the advertiser. If these are not consistent, doubts begin to arise in the public mind. What is the true image of the company? Which image should I believe? How should I react? If the picture is not clear, should I accept the company's offer? Do I want to do business with the company?

The case histories in this chapter were, for the most part, designated by those who sent them in as having image-building as their primary objective. It was the most popular in the CSPA competition. But, we must always remember that image-building is part of every sales promotion endeavor. We cannot help changing the way we appear to people by what we do and say. Be aware of this impact on people, and don't let the work that represents you have an unexpected influence on your public.

Getting the Folks to the Olympics

CLIENT:
Seagram Beverage Co., New York

AGENCY:
Siebel/Mohr, New York
(Marilyn F. Muller)

AWARDS:
1989 CSPA Award of Excellence
(Best of Category)

Seagram's Coolers was the leader in its category—but with only a slight lead—as its marketers looked ahead to the peak summer selling season. Its market share of the growing wine cooler category was 33.3 percent, with Bartles & Jaymes close behind with 31.3 percent.

Seagram's strategy for the upcoming summer season was to develop and implement an innovative, main-stream continuity program with national interest, and it picked a theme that only a category leader could undertake. This was built around the effort to pay for one parent of every member of the United States Olympic squad to go to Korea to attend the games. Called the Send the Families ™/American Team Family Fund, the program was based on the premise that trade and consumer excitement, and participation with a strong, American-based goodwill cause, were key to a successful and impactful peak season promotion.

A variety of merchandising materials was prepared for different kinds of outlets. Supermarkets and other broad-based retailers were offered two sizes of mass merchandisers, some case cards, and an assortment of support materials, including shelf talkers, posters, consumer brochures, television viewing guides, and carton stuffers. On-premise outlets, like bars and restaurants, were offered table tents and countercards which held brochures and television guides. Posters were also offered, with special designs developed for ethnic markets. All retailers who participated were given decals to mount in their windows. The program's advertising directed consumers to look for these decals. Major national accounts that wished to tie in with the program, for example United Airlines and Marriott Hotels, were offered customized materials.

A special video sales tape was produced for distributors and their sales force, outlining the program and building their enthusiasm. Distributors who signed up were made members of the Distributors Advisory Board, and received a membership decal and certificate, as well as a series of framed and signed lithographs created especially for the program by illustrator Bernie Fuchs.

The consumer aspect of the program was concentrated around three holiday weekends—Memorial Day, the Fourth of July, and Labor Day—when consumption of this product category is at a peak. The concentration during Memorial Day was on the series of fine arts posters, which were available with purchases. A free brochure described the poster offer, explained what the Send the Families program was all about, and listed some theme merchandise which could be ordered, with proceeds going to the fund. All consumers who made a purchase were given a Contributor Decal.

On July 4, the consumer was offered a refund on the purchase of a half-case or more of Seagram's Coolers, and he could contribute all or part of the refund to the program. On Labor Day, just prior to the Olympic Games, the consumer was offered a free guide to viewing the games on television. Since Seagram's was the exclusive wine cooler advertiser on the program, this helped build an audience for the spots.

One of the important supporting activities, which went on throughout the summer, was the development of the World's Largest Bon Voyage Card, which was to be presented to the group of parents as they assembled in Los Angeles for their trip to Seoul. The card traveled to 30 cities, gathering signatures and good will messages, as well as lots of good publicity in local and national media. While the number of signatures on the card went well over the 10,000 mark, other consumers, in markets where the Bon Voyage Tour did not go, added their signatures to smaller display cards.

Approximately 140,000 consumers participated in the case rebate program, and the average purchase went up to more than three 4-packs per purchase. The program obtained remarkable press coverage, with nearly 400 million impressions in monitored new media coverage. The estimated cost of making this number of impressions in paid media is somewhere between $7 and $10 million. And most important, more than 500 athletes were able to have a parent on hand to observe their participation in the Olympic Games.

The sell-in brochure outlined the entire promotion and showed retailers all its elements.

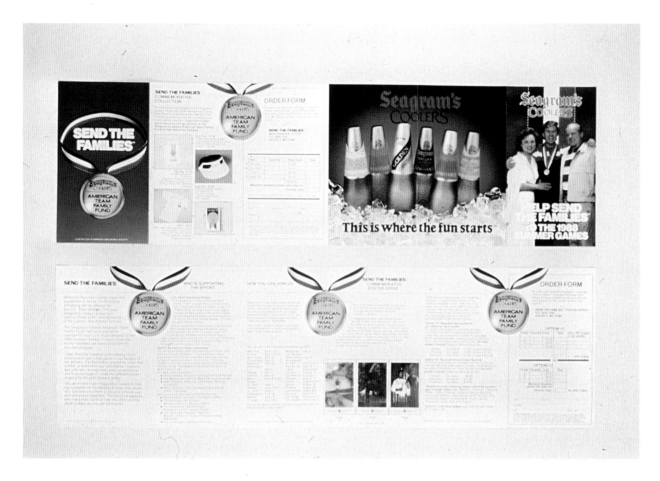

A large header was furnished for mass displays of six packs.

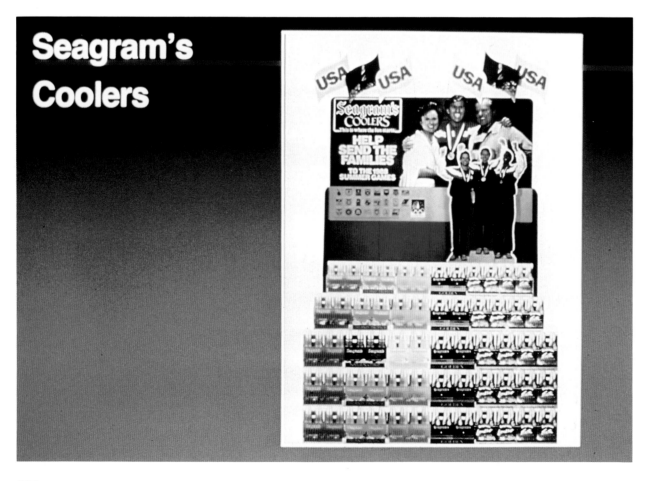

Here the offer was a trip to Europe to visit the 1992 Olympic cities. All three of these displays held take-one boxes with leaflets and order blanks for the promotional items.

The three specially-commissioned posters that were produced for the promotion.

A medal on a ribbon was used to reward cooperating retailers, and was also available to consumers.

Promotional material distributed to consumers, including the leaflet in the take-one box.

A Bon Voyage card greeted the parents as they assembled at the airport for their departure to Seoul.

Promotion is More Than Talk

CLIENT:

Bell Atlantic Corp., Arlington, VA
(Chris Clouser)

AGENCY:
Devon Direct, Malvern, PA
(Ron Greene, Jim Perry)

AWARD:
ECHO Award nominee

A good advertising campaign is even better and more effective when it is given promotional support. That was the experience of Bell Atlantic Corp., a company providing telephone and related services in Pennsylvania, Maryland, Delaware, New Jersey, Virginia, West Virginia, and the District of Columbia.

Bell Atlantic, the parent company of operating companies in these key areas, was about to introduce an advertising campaign with the theme "We're More than Just Talk." The company felt it was critical to introduce the new campaign to its key customers on a personal level, before the campaign hit the mass media. It believed that with the power of an integrated mass media and direct marketing approach, it could achieve greater impact from its new advertising campaign.

Telephone companies, in today's telecommunications world, offer broader and more complex services than ever before. Since they are competing in many of these new areas with a wide variety of different companies, it is often difficult for the public to keep track of the services that different companies provide. It was important that Bell's new advertising campaign, and the new corporate image it was presenting, stand out and be readily understood.

that Bell's new advertising campaign, and the new corporate image it was presenting, stand out and be readily understood.

The main piece of the campaign was an oversized self-mailer that presented a new image and inroduced the new campaign. It described, in a well-illustrated way, the many companies and services that comprise Bell Atlantic, and contained the two lead ads in the campaign. These ads were reproduced in full size for maximum impact.

The entire customer base received this mailing, as well as employee and special groups, such as communication consultants and press people. The oversized dimensions of the first-class mailing piece established an immediate presence in the mailbox and made sure that the piece wasn't over-looked. Its copy and design was kept short and simple, so attention would be focused on the key issue— the company's capabilities.

Special segments of the audience were isolated and special pieces were included to personalize the mailings. For example, customers in areas that could provide special services, like Call Waiting or Call Forwarding, received a piece providing information on these add-on services. Employees and key customers received a personal letter from Ray Smith, president and chief executive officer; financial officers got a cover letter from Philip Campbell, vice chairman and chief financial officer; the media's cover letter was signed by Chris Clouser, vice president of corporate relations and advertising.

The results of this particular program and its objectives are hard to measure, but Bell Atlantic feels that it provided its employees and key customers with a special preview of its new image, and enhanced the effect of its advertising campaign. Although direct order generation was not the primary objective of the program, it did bring in orders at a level exceeding any other form of advertising then in progress.

Blah,

It's Time To Let America Know... We're More Than Just Talk!

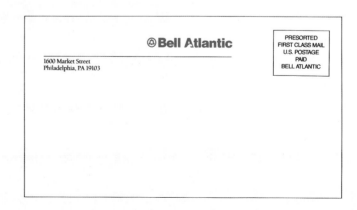

**Special Preview
For Bell Atlantic Customers**

Some time after the first mailing and the appearance of the ads, a recap brochure was sent to all business subscribers.

We're More Than Just Talk.^{SM}

Ⓐ **Bell of Pennsylvania**

Ⓐ **C&P Telephone**

Ⓐ **Diamond State Telephone**

Ⓐ **New Jersey Bell**

Ⓐ **Bell Atlantic**

Ⓐ **Bell Atlantic**

KEEPING DRIVERS SEEING GREEN
C&P Telephone provides the signalling facilities that coordinate traffic lights in Newport News, Va. to best meet the needs of motorists during the morning and evening rush hours.

provides Philadelphia with 9-1-1 Enhanced Service. When residents dial the emergency number, their name and location are automatically communicated to emergency services in the immediate area. They get help when they need it most.

And when Independence Blue Cross of Philadelphia needed a new mainframe system, disk and tapedrive and storage equipment — they worked with Bell of Pennsylvania's affiliate, Bell Atlantic Systems Leasing.

Bell of Pennsylvania is helping companies manage their information and grow in many other creative ways. Among them is our Bell Atlantic LANgate^{SM} service that can help turn your office phone system into a private data network.

Ⓐ C&P Telephone

Serving the unique communications needs of the nation's capital — as well as the neighboring states of Maryland, Virginia and West Virginia — is an enormous challenge. One

GIVING PEACE A CHANCE
In December of 1987, history was made. Leaders of great nations met. Communications were provided for the delegations. With the help of C&P Telephone, a summit was broadcast to the world over 45,000 feet of cable, nearly 1,200 dial-tone lines and 83 video links.

that the companies comprising C&P Telephone face and meet every day, just as they have for more than a century . . . providing quality phone service for over 4-million government, business and residential customers. But that's only one reason why C&P Telephone is vital to the region it serves.

For example, when President Bush took the oath of office on Inauguration Day, the world was able to see and hear it on over 100 video circuits and 1000 audio and data circuits installed by C&P Telephone. Both words and pictures travelled over more than 276,000 feet of Bell Atlantic fiber optic lines.

And other members of the Bell Atlantic family can offer C&P customers a host of important products and services.

JUST WHAT THE DOCTOR ORDERED
When the Johns Hopkins Medical Institution wanted better control over voice and data communications, they turned to C&P. By combining a Bell Atlantic LANgate^{SM} local area network with an Integrated Services Digital Network, C&P provided Hopkins with the basis for an information management system that, when fully developed, will allow physicians to quickly access patient records, charts, lab reports and prescription services right from their offices.

We're More Than Just Talk.^{SM}

Panic Can Produce
Prized Promotion

CLIENT:
3M-Riker Laboratories, St. Paul
(Diane Evenson)

AGENCY:
Hedstrom-Blessing Inc.,
Minneapolis
(Becky McManus, Susan Gustafson,
Richard Pynn, Andrea Roads)

AWARD:
Exhibitor's Sizzle Award

Sometimes pressure of time turns out well, and here is one example. Three days before 3M-Riker's promotion concepts had to go before the management of the annual meeting of the American Association of Family Physicians for approval, the selected vendor came in with nothing. In a panic, the company turned to Hedstrom/Blessing and asked for help. The agency came through with three concepts, and the mime idea was chosen.

It was a direct mail promotion, with a colorful mailer going out to all pre-registered physicians, and carried the theme "I left my heart in San Francisco," the site of the conference, as the only copy on its front cover. It invited all recipients to visit the 3M-Riker booth to attend a delightful mime performance, and to bring the mailing piece for a special, but unnamed, memento.

The performance was, indeed, delightful, and particularly appropriate for a show that saw many spouses and children accompanying physicians to the show. Everybody who attended was given a heart-shaped balloon, which soon became a prominent item bobbing around the show floor. Those who remembered to present their mailing piece got an additional gift—a T-shirt using the art from the mailing piece, plus the words, "I got mime in San Francisco."

An astounding 80 percent of the mailing pieces were presented at the booth, and 2,400 T-shirts were distributed. Over 200 leads were generated, resulting in a very satisfactory new physician contact.

We're up to some real, live fun that's sure to stir some whispers. *And you're invited!*

The T-shirt picked up the artwork from the mailing piece, and added a cute slogan.

The self mailer, 8½"x11", was sent
out by first class mail. Its front cover
was a full-color illustration.

We'll capture your heart in San Francisco.

Visit the Riker/3M Booth and see a show within a show!

There's a lot to be said for visiting San Francisco. Then again, some of its sights and sensations are enough to leave you speechless!

During the AAFP show, we're hoping to take your breath away for at least a moment with delightful and entertaining mime performances, appearing throughout each day.

But that's not all the fun we'll be having at Booth #1608!

All visitors will leave with a special mime show memento, (but— mum's the word!) **Plus, if you present this card at our booth, we'll give you a bonus surprise!**

See what we're talking about, or not talking about, in September. And, you will have the opportunity to talk to our sales representatives about any of our fine Riker products:

- Theolair™-SR ● Disalcid®
- Norgesic® Forte/Norflex®
- Tambocor®

Hope to see you there!

The 39th Annual Convention of the American Academy of Family Physicians

September 14-17, 1987
The Moscone Center, San Francisco

Riker Laboratories, Inc./3M
Booth #1608

The inside spread continued the heart motif, and urged recipients to bring the mailer to the Riker booth. An astounding 80 percent of them actually showed up!

Getting a Head Start on Banking

CLIENT:
Williamsburgh Savings Bank/
Republic National Bank,
New York
(Dave Rosen, Nancy Moses)

AGENCY:
The Marketing Department Inc.,
New York
(Alan Toman, Suzanne Ford,
Sharon Palatnik)

AWARDS:
Promotion Marketing Association
of America, 1989 Gold Reggie
American Marketing Association,
1989 SPIRE Award
Financial Advertising &
Marketing Association, Town
Crier Award

Banks are formidable places, especially for kids, but if you can get a kid involved, you may have achieved the beginning of a life-long relationship. That was the point of the Bank for Kids promotion developed when the Republic National Bank acquired the Williamsburgh Savings Bank, 138 years old and one of the largest in the New York area.

It started in one of the Williamsburgh branches located in a shopping center on Long Island. It was a bank-within-a-bank for kids up to 17 years of age, featuring its own special teller (a bank retiree), and extended banking hours. Within the self-contained facility were banking games, a computer, and an interactive video to help teach kids more about the value of savings. Kids were issued their own make-believe ATM card which gave them entrance to the facility.

The four-week promotion was launched in the mall with a back-to-school sweepstakes that offered instant prizes, twice-weekly drawings of $25 gift certificates at participating merchants, and six grand prizes, including a $500 shopping spree.

Merchants participated by providing displays for Banks for Kids, including a 4-foot cutout of "Billy," the promotion's spokesman. This was equipped with a kid-activated voice box that described the sweepstakes, and by distributing Bank for Kids shopping bags. Cooperating merchants were listed in Bank for Kids materials, were included in the gift certificates, and were authorized to issue a coupon with each purchase of $25 or more which could be turned in at the Bank for a personalized picture button.

The promotion resulted in the opening of thousands of special accounts, exceeding objectives by over 200 percent. In addition, 15 percent of the new kids' accounts resulted in opening of new accounts by their parents, and this figure is continuing to grow. One quarter of the mall merchants participated in the promotion, and 25 percent of these opened new business accounts with Williamsburgh.

A folder, written in simple language, explained the plan to kids and parents. The last page was an official application, to be signed by a kid and countersigned by a parent or guardian.

Official Application

YES! I'm interested in becoming a BANK for KIDS member. Please send me more information.
(Please print neatly)

My name is _____

Address _____

City _____ State _____ Zip _____

Phone number_____

My birthday is ___/___/___ Age_____

School_____ Grade _____

Social Security number _____ _____ _____

My Mom's name is _____

My Dad's name is _____

This is the part your Mom, Dad, or Legal Guardian has to sign:

Guarantee/Consent Form

I am the parent or legal guardian of_____ (Minor) who is under 18 years of age and who is opening a BANK for KIDS Savings Account ("Account") at The Williamsburgh Savings Bank (Williamsburgh). If Williamsburgh opens this Account for the Minor, I agree to pay Williamsburgh for any fees, penalties, losses, damages, claims or costs which Williamsburgh may have to pay, or may be entitled to receive, because the Minor has refused to comply with the Account Agreement or has refused to pay any of these amounts.

_____
Signature of Minor's Parent   Date
or Legal Guardian

Williamsburgh
SAVINGS BANK
A Republic New York Corporation Bank

➡️

Benjamin: All you need to open your own **BANK for KIDS** Account is:

Billy: $2.00 (or more, of course!)

Benjamin: Your parent's or guardian's signature,

Bernice: And your Social Security number.

And a ride to the Bank!

Billy: If your parents need to know more about **BANK for KIDS**, just call this number: (212) 221-6056 in NYC or 1-800-522-5214 outside NYC, or tear off the attached application form and bring it, or send it, to **BANK for KIDS!**

COME JOIN THE GANG!!

CAN'T WAIT TO MEET YOU!

SEE YOU SOON AT

bank for kids

OUR VERY OWN BANK!!

Williamsburgh
SAVINGS BANK
A Republic New York Corporation Bank

bank for kids ℠

And How It Works...
for you and your money!

WBFK 07 (6-88)

FOR KIDS ONLY!

No Grownups Allowed!

It's EASY to become a member of the **BANK for KIDS** gang!

If you're a kid, 17 years old or younger, you can open your very own savings account at **BANK for KIDS** with a minimum of only $2... and watch your money grow!

Look inside and see!

Billy: Hi! Meet the **BANK for KIDS** Gang! We're here to tell you all about **BANK for KIDS**, and how *you* can become a member!

Bernice: When you open an account at **BANK for KIDS**, it has *your* name on it - and it's your private property. You can put money in and take it out...as often as you like!

Billy: It doesn't cost anything to have a **BANK for KIDS** Savings Account it's free!

Benjamin: And while your money is in your Account at **BANK for KIDS**, it "earns interest".

Billy: That means that the Bank gives you extra money (5 1/2 cents for every dollar - and sometimes more as a special bonus) just to thank you for being a **BANK for KIDS** member!

Bernice: You can save money for a new computer game...

Benjamin: ...a vacation or a good book...

Billy: ...a baseball glove or a birthday present for your mom...

...or a steak for your dog!

Everybody: Anything you want!

Billy: When you open a **BANK for KIDS** account, you get:

Benjamin: Your own special **BANK for KIDS** Savings Account passbook, with your balance (how much money is in your account) recorded in it, every time it changes.

Bernice: A special **BANK for KIDS** Membership Card which entitles you to special **BANK for KIDS** privileges!

Billy: You can come to **BANK for KIDS** during regular banking hours, and also during special times one day every week when the Bank is open just for kids!

Benjamin: And guess what? At the Bank, there are lots of games and videos to play with and learn from - designed especially for **BANK for KIDS** members!

Bernice: And you get a *stunning* **BANK for KIDS** T-shirt!

Oh good, something to chew.

Billy: Invitations to great **BANK for KIDS** parties... Valentine's Day, Halloween or other fun holidays!

A NOTE TO PARENTS AND OTHER GROWNUPS

You may have noticed that the prevailing attitude about saving and spending money has changed since you opened your first bank account, perhaps when you were a child. At our Bank, we're concerned that our children are growing up in a country whose per capita savings rate is among the lowest of all the developed nations in the world.

We'd like children to understand that they can do more with their money than just spend it. We believe that our corporate mission to protect our customers and their assets applies especially to the children of the communities we serve. We've decided to invest some time and effort in teaching children about financial responsibility - by giving it to them.

At **BANK for KIDS**, a child can save for anything he or she decides is an appropriate goal. It's all up to the individual child. There are no fees and a minimum balance of only $2.00 is required. A child can come to the Bank during regular hours and also at special times reserved only for **BANK for KIDS** members. At **BANK for KIDS**, there are educational games and programs about a wide range of subjects, including basic money skills.

If you think your child is ready to begin learning the value of saving, in a fun, inspiring atmosphere, we're glad to be able to welcome you both to **BANK for KIDS**.

It is necessary to have a Social Security number to open a bank account. If your child doesn't have one, call your nearest Social Security Office. Make sure your child has a birth certificate or other proof of age, identity, and citizen or alien status.

➡️

A variety of promotional materials was available, ranging from a shopping bag to a life-size cutout character, who spoke to passersby via a kid-activated voice box.

Window banners were used by all cooperating merchants.

Attractive shopping bags were also used to call attention to the new installation.

Counter cards which held copies of the folder were used both at the bank, and in cooperating merchants' stores.

This 4-foot cutout of Billy had a sound message which was activated whenever a person came within its range.

Quality Merchandise
Sells a Quality Product

CLIENT:
Benson & Hedges; Philip Morris
USA, New York
(Marla Antonoff, Ashley O'Neil)

AGENCY:
Wells, Rich, Greene, New York
(Arnold Weintraub, Joel Pennay)
Communications Diversified
Promotion Agency
(Ron Wall)

AWARD:
Promotion of the Month, June
1988, *Promo Magazine*

One way of building a quality image is by being associated with quality merchandise. Benson & Hedges, the seventh largest selling brand of cigarettes, wanted to encourage not only trial purchasers, but to generate continuity of purchase. The medium chosen for this promotion was an elegent catalog, entitled "Quality Choices," that offered more than 40 luxurious items at a substantial discount. Each order had to be accompanied by proofs of purchase of two cartons of Benson & Hedges cigarettes.

The 14-page, full color catalog was distributed in magazines, by direct mail, and at the point-of-sale. It ran as an insert in April issues of *Time, Newsweek,* and *People*; in the May issues of *Cosmopolitan, Elle, GQ, Metropolitan Home, Money,* and other magazines with a total circulation of 18 million. Forty thousand of the catalogs were mailed directly to a list of some 40,000 upscale smokers. But the major impact, perhaps, was that of some 17,000 retail outlets in which were installed self-shipping displays in two sizes. One held 30 cartons;

the other 60. What helped move product from these displays was the premium, a good ballpoint pen, attached to each carton and given away with the carton purchase. Copies of the "Quality Choices" catalog were also available at the displays.

Excitement was added to the promotion by a sweepstakes open only to retailers and to the Philip Morris sales force. This was announced by a folder which was included in the sell-in brochure. The entry form was a simple business reply card. The PM sales rep made out and mailed in a card, giving his name and the name of the store manager each time he successfully sold the promotion. Each of the seven regional sales divisions had a set of three prizes, drawn from the Quality Choices catalog, and 1,000 gift certificates were awarded, each good for a weekend for two at a Hilton hotel. Matching prizes were given to the retailers and to the PM sales representatives whose names were on the winning cards.

Customer response to the catalog was greater than expected, with orders coming in asking for several items at once, averaging more than $100 per order. In addition, the promotion received off-shelf display for up to two weeks in 17,000 outlets.

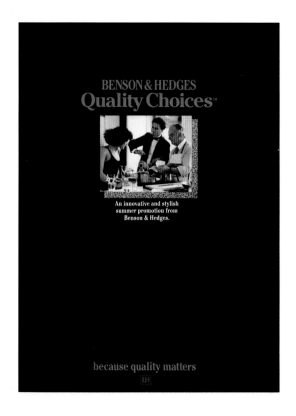

A glossy folder was prepared for selling the promotion. It contained details of the promotion, a sample catalog of premiums, and an entry blank that entered the store manager and the salesman in the sweepstakes.

Each carton carried an on-pack premium of a fine ballpoint pen. The catalog was widely available.

150

The countercard display held individual packs of Benson & Hedges, and a supply of gift catalogs.

30 Deal Display

This self-shipping display held 30 cartons of cigarettes, and promoted both the catalog and the ballpoint pen premium. A larger version held 60 cartons.

When Santa and Disney Work Together

CLIENT:
The Coca-Cola Co., Atlanta
(J. Tyler Taylor)

Within the multi-billion dollar soft drink industry, each market share point represents approximately $400 million in sales for any given brand. As a result, every battle won in the hard-fought "cola wars," has a very significant impact on the brand's growth, image, and profitability.

One of the most important battles in this year-long war takes place during the fourth quarter holiday season. This period is one of the single largest volume-building opportunities of the year.

In 1988, it was apparent that if Coca-Cola Classic maximized its opportunities during the fourth quarter, it would be able to gain significantly on its nearest competitor, Pepsi-Cola, both in Nielsen share, which represents supermarket movement, and in overall product case sales.

The way to widen the gap between the two rivals was, in the eyes of the Coca-Cola promotion people, to increase the sales of Coca-Cola Classic with women in the 18 to 49 age bracket. A tie-in with one of the strongest family entertainment companies in the world, Disney/Disney Home Video, was a chance to win a home entertainment package that was unavailable in retail stores. This would not only lead to sales, but would also help to increase the size and duration of displays in supermarkets, which is the surest way to increase sales.

It was a simple sweepstakes, with five grand prizes, each a complete home video collection of Disney classic movies and cartoons, more than 250 titles! A set of six of the tapes, including Disney's 1988 release, Cinderella, was the first prize, of which 5,000 were awarded.

The promotion was given extensive support, both through publicity, in national television advertising, as well as local radio and television commercials, with some merchandising sweepstakes in selected markets. Retailers were given material to incorporate in their own ads in support of the promotion.

The objective was to get displays installed. These were built around the familiar Disney characters, and carried entry blanks for the national sweepstakes, which, in some stores, were supplemented by local events in which the customer could win "Video Six Packs." There was also a separate, but related sweepstakes just for children 12 years and under.

The promotion was well accepted by retailers, with 80 percent of the eligible stores supporting the event with product displays. As a result, the Nielsen figure for the December/January period showed that Coca-Cola Classic grew by 0.4 percent, while Pepsi dropped 0.2 percent. This growth enabled Coca-Cola classic to reach its highest share since the brand was reintroduced in 1985.

The cover of the sell-in brochure featured Santa and some of the best-known Disney characters, along with the familiar logos of the two organizations.

The large stack header used the same Santa figure, as well as a group of his friends from Disney.

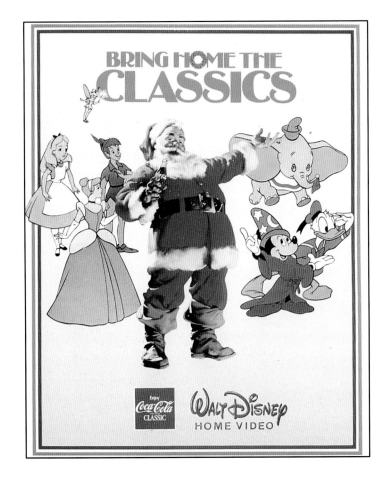

A Promotion with a Cause

CLIENT:
Members Only, New York
(Maia L. Hauser)

AWARDS:
1989 CSPA Award of Excellence
(Finalist)

Members Only has been known for a long time for its cause-related promotions, especially for its 1986 drug abuse campaign. In 1988, the company became acutely aware that 81 million eligible voters chose not to vote in the 1984 presidential election, resulting in a paltry 50 percent turn-out. It recognized the immediate and pressing need for a broad national campaign that would encourage people to register and to vote in the upcoming presidential election. Working with the League of Women Voters, Members Only began a far-reaching campaign that included national and local advertising, local registration events, prizes and celebrity appearances. The company's entire national advertising budget for the Fall season was devoted to this cause, using the theme "There is no Excuse not to Vote."

The objectives were defined early. The first was the decision to address an issue of immediate importance. This should be done to reinforce the corporate identity as a leader in cause-related marketing. The sales objectives were to increase trade support in the spring, when retailers are stocking fall merchandise, and to increase consumer support in the fall during the height of the year's selling seaosn.

The strategy was to create an integrated national and local campaign that would include advertising, sales promotion, event marketing, and public relations. The national aspect of the promotion was built around an unusual, emotionally gripping television campaign that would focus attention on the issue of voting rather than on the two candidates. The local aspect was to create exciting traffic-building events in department stores that would motivate people to register to vote and to obtain non-partisan voting information at tables administered and staffed by the League.

Another event was a sweepstakes with the top prize being a trip for two to Washington, DC, and utilizing American Airlines, the Grand Hyatt Washington Hotel, and a $500 shopping spree on Master Card. All three of these companies donated their prizes in return for visibility to a target group of department store shoppers. At many of the events, Members Only sponsored old-fashioned parties, complete with live bands, dancing, hotdogs, gifts and prizes.

Wherever possible, Members Only helped to support related events that urged greater election participation. An example was the Kid's Convention co-sponsored in Los Angeles by May Company. This involved Kid's Caucuses at schools, voting at the stores for a Kid's Convention Platform while their parents registered, and a Kid's Convention at Universal Studios, attended by 2,500 kids.

Independent men's stores were invited to participate in the event. While they might not be able to get in as deeply as could the major department stores, some 1,200 Voting Program Kits were mailed to retailers. These contained materials which would allow the smaller stores to conduct their own events and profit from the promotion.

The program produced outstanding results in all areas. The advertising was so dramatic and striking that it was covered as a news item by major television networks. Trade support was far more than expected, with many stores so pleased with the program that they voluntarily paid for additional support. Consumer support was unprecedented, with about 100,000 people taking part in the sweepstakes, and over 10,000 people actually registering. And of course, it didn't hurt that sales of Members Only products were 23 percent higher in the Fall of 1988 than a year earlier.

The campaign was kicked off with a letter from the president of the League of Women Voters to department store presidents. She urged them to become good corporate citizens in their own communities by taking a leadership position locally in the Members Only/League of Women Voters program. She informed them that representatives of the two organizations would call on them soon to talk about the problem and how they could contribute to its solution. Finally, she stressed that this was not a fund-raising effort, emphasizing that Members Only had already financed the effort, and what was needed was local support in the way of time, effort, and space.

The two organizations made follow-up calls, and arranged meetings with store executives, merchandisers, advertising, publicity, and special events people, to ensure that there would be a totally integrated communications program. At these meetings, the dramatic national advertising campaign was outlined, along with a number of ideas for events in which the stores could participate.

Realistically, voter registration campaigns could not be expected to draw great attendance so special events were developed with each store to build traffic. Typical of these events were NFL Nights at which leading players appeared, urging their fans to become informed, to register, and later to vote. This was a natural, since Members Only was an NFL sponsor. Participants included the Redskins' Doug Williams, the Vikings' Wade Wilson, and New York Giants Joe Morris and Karl Nelson. Local sports-casters and deejays participated as hosts, helping to promote the events on air. These football events were advertised locally in tailored campaigns, and helped to attract young men who represent the lowest voter turnout.

50% VOTER TURNOUT ISN'T WHAT THEY HAD IN MIND.

There is no excuse not to vote.

MEMBERS ONLY
Apparel And Other Fine Products.

50% VOTER TURNOUT ISN'T EXACTLY WHAT THEY HAD IN MIND.

There is no excuse not to vote.

Promotion
with Innovation

CLIENT:
Zenith Data Systems, Mount
Prospect, IL

AGENCY:
Impact, Chicago
(Marion Black-Ruffin)

When your budget is limited, you have to turn to imagination and ingenuity to achieve your goal. The "Masters of Innovation Competition," produced for Zenith Data Systems by Impact, a Chicago sales promotion agency, is a prime example of innovative sales promotion strategy and execution. Using classic promotion techniques amidst a state-of-the-art, high technology backdrop, creates a challenging and compelling offer for consumers in the growing personal computer category.

While Zenith Data Systems is one of the "big eight" manufacturers of personal computers, it is operating in a field dominated by the clout and achievement of IBM and the creativity and showmanship of Apple. It has kept itself competitive by selectively innovating various PC products and offering them at a competitive price.

It cannot outspend the two category giants. In fact, its sales and marketing strategy has been to sell directly to large companies, and avoid the traditional distribution and dealership system and its connected costs; the strategy has paid off well. ZDS has become a major supplier of PCs to the Federal government, and has also carved a niche in academic/educational circles, in spite of the that it gets little or no displays in college bookstores or local PC dealerships.

It was now time, management thought, to make an impact on the academic market, reinforce its image of computer innovation, and bolster the efforts of its small sales force and its student sales representative network.

To achieve this objective, Zenith set up a contest that was offered in over 1,500 college campuses nationwide. Called the "Masters of Innovation Competition," the promotion called upon entrants to describe, in a two- to five-page paper, how they developed or used software for their personal computer to creatively address a problem or task within their field of study.

Entries could be made in one of five fields of study, Business, Liberal Arts and Science, Education, Engineering/ Computer Science, Fine and Applied Arts. Separate contests were run for students and for faculty/staff members, with three prizes awarded in each of these fields, making 30 prizes in all. The first prize was a $5,000 ZDS computer package to the winner, with an additional $5,000 of computer equipment to the department of which the winner belonged. The other two prizes were $3,500 and $2,000 Zenith computer packages.

The program was announced to the on-campus audiences through point-of-sale materials in student unions, bookstores, computer labs and departmental offices. Posters, counter cards, mobiles and tent cards were used. In addition, direct mail was sent to students, and advertising was run in select education trade publications.

To enter, students and others were asked to call a toll free number to receive an entry packet that explained the competition and spelled out the rules. This unusual technique was chosen to make sure that the materials got into the right hands, and to build a mailing list. In addition, this unusual and prolonged entry format provided an overtone of seriousness and earnestness to the program, enhancing the ZDS commitment to innovation and its search for technological excellence from the entrants.

All applications were judged by a special review committee consisting of editors from *Classroom Computer Learning* and *Technology on Campus*, as well as key representatives from each of the five academic fields, the computer industry and the computer publishing industry.

The program has proved to be a major success. Over 6,000 entry packets were distributed to students, faculty and staff, in hundreds of colleges and universities across the country. Releases on the winners were sent to the appropriate campus and local newspapers, gaining further exposure for Zenith.

Variations on the basic piece of art, a group of heads silhouetted against a portrait of Albert Einstein, were used on posters, counter cards, and table tents, many of which carried pockets for entry instruction folders.

When Things are Bad, They're Good!

CLIENT:
Pepsi-Cola Canada, Toronto
(John Tevlin, Joe Palombo, Tony Milina)

AGENCY:
Marketing & Promotion Group, Toronto
(Leo Slocombe)

When Pepsi International got involved with Michael Jackson, its affiliate companies found that it paid to get themselves involved, too. In Canada, the affiliate company built its promotion around a radio contest. The objective was to make the target market aware that Pepsi was supporting Michael Jackson, and persuade the young customers to see all four parts of a special television commercial that the company was airing on a strong youth-oriented program.

The commercial was indeed unique. Built around a story involving the popular singer, the four-minute commercial was to be aired as four individual minutes during a nationwide broadcast of the Grammy Awards show. This would be the only time this commercial would be aired.

In each market area, a single radio station was chosen for the promotion, based on how well the station reached the particular audience Pepsi wanted to reach. Newspaper advertising was used to build the audience for the campaign, but this was backed up with bottle necktags, tear-off pads, shelf talkers, and posters. Each of these items specified the local station that was running the contest, the television channel that would be broadcasting the Pepsi/Jackson commercial, and the offer of the grand prize of a trip to London for two, during which the winner would attend a Michael Jackson concert.

Entering the contest was simple. An entry form was available at most stores, along with three proofs of purchase of Pepsi. For some weeks prior to the Grammy show, names were drawn from the entry blanks sent in to the station, and the winners were awarded "Bad in Britain" T-shirts and cassettes of the

Jackson album "Bad." Announcements of the winners were made on the air. But the grand prize, the trip to London, had to wait until after the Grammy Show. To qualify for the prize, the person selected had to answer a question about the 4-part commercial broadcast the night before. If he or she couldn't give an answer that showed that he or she had watched, the station kept on picking until it found someone who had.

Each participating radio station awarded its own grand prize. A total of 50 trips to London were given away, with Wardair supplying a large part of the air fare in return for being listed as a participant in the promotion.

On-premise consumption of Pepsi was encouraged by offering patrons of its food service accounts an opportunity to qualify for similar prizes, but the on-premise promotion went under the title "Live in London," in order to keep the two promotions separate. This had its own display pieces, like table tents, that encouraged entries. Patrons simply sent in a form which they were given with each purchase.

The entry form used the same artwork that was used throughout, and was imprinted with the local information.

A shelf talker, with space for local pricing, was imprinted with the local cooperating station.

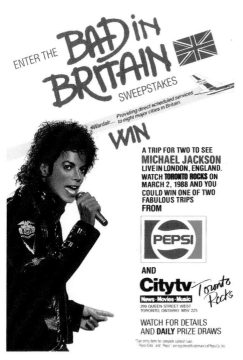

Promoting a Hidden Service

CLIENT:
Eastman Kodak Co.,
Photofinishing Systems Division,
Rochester, NY
(Robert Weir, Kathy Udavchak)

AGENCY:
Eison-Freeman Inc., Paramus, NJ
(Patricia Little, Joe Tschida, Lee Blumner)

The Kodak Colorwatch system is the photo industry's market leader in photofinishing, with a 70 percent share of the market. However, most consumers were not aware of the role that the Colorwatch system and Eastman Kodak played in their satisfaction. In addition to enhancing the Colorwatch image among consumers, Kodak wanted to reinforce the value to dealers of being a Colorwatch system member.

The 100th anniversary of the introduction of snapshot photography coincided with the promotion, providing a natural backdrop to highlight Kodak's enduring affiliation with photography and its expertise in the field. The promotion was designed to involve both consumers and dealers.

Photofinishers were supplied with game cards that they placed in each finishing envelope, to be delivered to the consumer when he picked up his finished work. The consumer scratched off any two of eight "snapshots" on the card. If he revealed two dollar signs, he would win $100,000. Prizes offered in an instant-win bonus box included a chance to win a Ford Taurus sedan, 10 vacation trips to Walt Disney World, and 1,000 Kodak 35mm camera outfits. In addition, each card carried a coupon valued at 50¢ off any two rolls of Kodak film.

The promotion was widely advertised on network TV and in publications like *USA Weekend, Parade,* and *People,* with ad slicks for dealers. The advertising, as well as the point-of-purchase materials, featured Bill Cosby, which reinforced Kodak's national campaign. Window banners, counter cards, and mobiles were offered to the dealers.

Based on a post-promotion consumer study, the event resulted in a 16 percent increase in consumer awareness that their dealer was a member of the Kodak Colorwatch system. Seventy-three percent reported receiving game cards, and 54 percent had played the game.

A coupon, with eight scratch-off areas, was put in each order returned to the consumer. The tear-off section to the right offered a discount on more film.

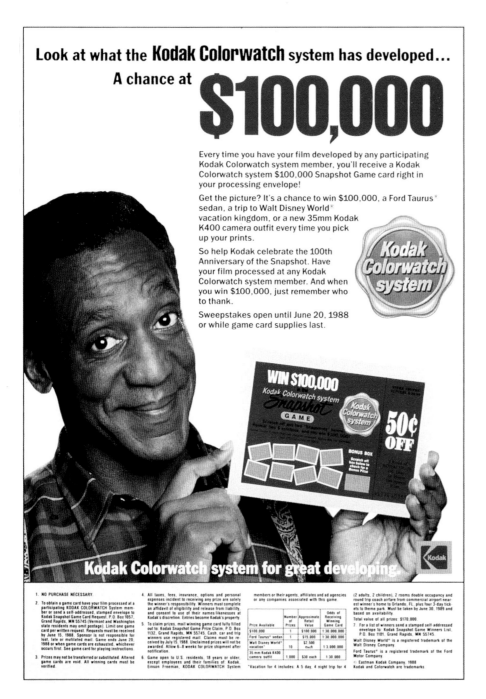

Look at what the **Kodak Colorwatch** system has developed…
A chance at
$100,000

Every time you have your film developed by any participating Kodak Colorwatch system member, you'll receive a Kodak Colorwatch system $100,000 Snapshot Game card right in your processing envelope!

Get the picture? It's a chance to win $100,000, a Ford Taurus* sedan, a trip to Walt Disney World* vacation kingdom, or a new 35mm Kodak K400 camera outfit every time you pick up your prints.

So help Kodak celebrate the 100th Anniversary of the Snapshot. Have your film processed at any Kodak Colorwatch system member. And when you win $100,000, just remember who to thank.

Sweepstakes open until June 20, 1988 or while game card supplies last.

Kodak Colorwatch system for great developing.

Bill Cosby was featured holding the coupon in ads that appeared in national publications. Cosby was also used in network TV commercials.

The window banner made the grand prize offer even more prominent.

A counter card simply picked up the full-page ad.

Virtually the same elements, including the popular and ubiquitous Cosby, made up the mobile.

It Takes Promotion
to Sell Promotion

CLIENT:
Lucasfilm Ltd., Nicosia, CA
(Howard Roffman, Brad Weston,
Louise Riley)

AGENCY:
US Communications Corp.,
Minneapolis
(Corky Hall, Tanna Moore, Mike Zeman)

AWARDS:
1988 Silver Spire, American
Marketing Association

During the Summer of 1988, four major motion pictures were due for release, and since a major movie needs all the promotional help it can get, all four were in search of corporate tie-ins. This is the story of how one of them, "W-I-L-L-O-W", produced by George Lucas of Lucasfilms, with sales promotion agency US Communications Corp., achieved the goal. To get to the right companies and persuade them that one of these films would furnish the strongest tie-in with the most closely fitting demographic audience, and thus sell product for them, took a promotional campaign of its own.

The first step was to identify those product categories, and within them, those companies which would have the highest potential of accomplishing the objectives for image enhancement. A goal of three to five cooperating companies was set.

The first step was to make a presentation to each of these companies, outlining the past success of George Lucas' films, and what might be expected with "W-I-L-L-O-W". This was done in separate meetings at each company's location, using slides, videotapes and film clips.

If the promotion people seemed to be serious, they were invited to pay a visit to Skywalker Ranch, Lucas' headquarters, where they could meet the Lucas people and discuss in-depth, the opportunity this film would provide.

The film would be released in May, and the producer wanted promotional activity to continue at a steady level through August, so a calendar had to be developed to maintain continuous interest in the film, without conflicting with any of the sponsors, each of which had its own promotional objectives and calendar.

The campaign ended up with six cooperating manufacturers, whose campaigns consistently promoted the film as well as the individual objectives of each company. The series started off in May and June, working with a number of brands from Kraft Foods. June saw the addition of Jell-O, from General Foods, and Wendy's Fast Food Restaurants. Quaker Oats joined the group for June and July (*see separate story on Quaker's promotion in Chapter 4*), while Ziploc Sandwich Bags, from DowBrands, and Beatrice/Hunt Wesson's Peter Pan Peanut Butter promotions were held in August. All of these, with the exception of Wendy's, were developed by US Communications Corp. for Lucasfilm, while Wendy's was done directly by Lucasfilm, with the assistance of Marketing Equities, Inc.

Each of the corporate sponsors had its own "W-I-L-L-O-W" campaign, which included various combinations of free-standing inserts, premiums, special offers, and point-of-purchase displays. The total amount of marketing support was in excess of $50 million, which made it the largest and most fully integrated tie-in promotion with a film in the history of the industry.

A full color brochure used shots from the movies to introduce the excitement of the new film and its possibilities.

YOU REMEMBER STAR WARS® AND INDIANA JONES®.

Anyone for Fontana Candida?

CLIENT:
Fontana Candida Wine, imported by Brown-Forman Beverage Co., Louisville
(Bill Juckett, Rick Povill, Dinah Smiley, Saralinda Hicks)

AGENCY:
PriceWeber, Louisville
(Bill Swearingen)

AWARDS:
Promo of the Month, July 1988:
Promo Magazine

Fontana Candida is a versatile, Italian white wine with a lot of competition, from such familiar brands as Bolla, Lancers, Blue Nun, Mouton-Cadet, and others. Fontana is positioned as "the light sophisticated wine of Rome." In trying to reinforce the brand's Roman heritage and light taste, PriceWeber discovered that tennis aficianados are more likely to drink white wine than the average consumer. Fontana Candida capitalized on this association with a targeted promotion—the Fontana Candida Italian Open Sweepstakes. Consumers were invited to enter a tennis-oriented sweepstakes. The grand prize was an all-expense-paid trip for two to Rome, which included tickets to the Italian Open Tennis Tournament. Prizes also included 10 sets of Fila warmups, 25 Fila tennis rackets, and 100 Fila tennis visors.

In liquor stores and supermarkets, the sweepstakes was merchandised by cut case cards and shelf talker entry pads. One could also pick up entry forms at bars and lounges, with a special effort to target country clubs, tennis clubs, and other appropriate restaurant accounts. Table tents with entry forms were used to promote sale of the brand by the glass or bottle. These clubs were encouraged to sponsor their own tournaments, and use Fontana Candida to merchandise the tournament in Rome.

Thousands of entries were received, displays were widely used, and sales of the product jumped during the promotion period.

FONTANA CANDIDA

THE LIGHT, SOPHISTICATED WINE OF ROME

Tennis, Anyone?
PUT MORE SALES IN YOUR COURT WITH FONTANA CANDIDA'S ITALIAN OPEN SWEEPSTAKES.

Tennis, Fontana Candida and the Italian Open Sweepstakes...a natural combination for a great May promotion.

- Tennis players, compared to the average consumer, are significantly more likely to be wine consumers.*
- Fontana Candida's taste is the perfect match for today's active lifestyle...clean, light and refreshing.
- Add the excitement of Fontana Candida's Italian Open Sweepstakes promotion running concurrently with the May, 1988 Italian Open Tennis Tournament in Rome.

Rome's favorite white wine and Rome's famous tennis tournament. It's a perfect promotion for putting more sales in your court.

Plus, customers get the chance to win fabulous sweepstakes prizes.

Grand Prize.
Tickets for two to next year's Italian Open Tennis Tournament...with a one-week, all-expense-paid vacation in Rome (May, 1989).

Over 100 1st, 2nd, and 3rd Prize Winners.
One hundred thirty-five 1st, 2nd and 3rd place winners will receive outstanding prizes of Fila® tennis attire and equipment.

Cut Case Card.
Exciting design invites customers to enjoy Fontana Candida and enter the Italian Open Sweepstakes. Complete with 50 mail-in entry blanks and details about the fabulous sweepstakes prizes: tickets for two to the May, 1989 Italian Open Tennis Tournament in Rome; 10 sets of Fila tennis wear; 25 Fila tennis rackets; and 100 Fila visors.
Dimensions: 17"W x 35"H (including 10" tongue)
Code #330-3080

Shelf Card.
Italian Open Sweepstakes excitement at the shelf. Each Shelf Card complete with 50 mail-in entry blanks.
Dimensions: 8½"W x 3"H
Code #330-3090

The full color sell-in sheet illustrates the cut case card and the shelf card on one side. The other side gives the details of the sweepstakes, and included a profit calculator.

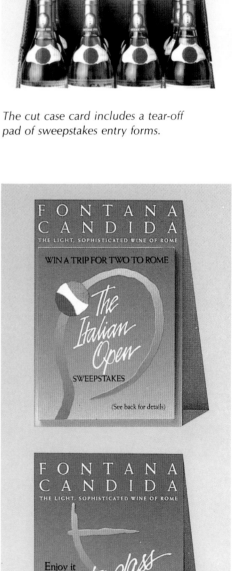

The cut case card includes a tear-off pad of sweepstakes entry forms.

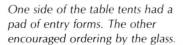

One side of the table tents had a pad of entry forms. The other encouraged ordering by the glass.

169

A British Promotion

CLIENT:
Guinness Import Co., Stamford, CT

(Don Blaustein, Declan Maguire, Greg Kelly, Cindy Shore)

AGENCY:
Sims Freeman O'Brien, Elmsford, NY

(Ian Jacob, Mickie Miller, Karen D'Angelo, Howard Temmer, Colin Cooke)

AWARDS:
1989 CSPA Award of Excellence (Finalist)
1988 SPIRE Bronze Award (Beverage Category)

When the appeal of your product is its illustrious heritage and its country of origin, you've clearly got a good base for a successful promotion. That was how the innovative "British Life" promotion platform for Guinness Import Co.'s Bass Ale got started.

Bass Ale is the leading British ale sold in the United States. However, it faced stiff competition from imported and domestic beers. To maintain its position, it sought a promotional strategy for the spring and fall of 1988 that would differentiate Bass Ale from its competitors; raise its brand awareness among consumers, wholesalers and retailers; encourage trial; increase distribution among existing accounts; and attain new distribution.

The two themed campaigns that were developed capitalized upon the reputation of the brand and its country of origin. The Spring 1988 campaign was entitled "Enjoy the British Country Life," and the Fall campaign, "Enjoy the British Sporting Life." The twin campaigns provided the Bass Ale brand themed promotional support materials that raised awareness among consumers, wholesalers, and retailers, while encouraging trial among non-Bass consumers. This resulted in increased distribution among existing accounts and a gain in new account distribution all across the United States.

In both campaigns, customers were offered discounts for multiple purchases, and exciting sweepstakes opportunities. Luxurious grand prize trips to Great Britain tied in with the overall promotion theme. For the Country Life phase, the other prizes were British snooker tables and croquet sets, while Camcorders were offered in the Sporting Life phase.

In package stores, beverage centers and supermarkets, cleverly-designed point-of-purchase materials were the main communication tools, cutting through the clutter with bold graphics and style. Colorful art was used in new ways on displays, table tents and bottle neckers. The Spring promotion featured a sophisticated fox hunt etching, and for the Fall, scenes from three traditional sporting events. A photograph of the product in an inviting pub setting was featured in both campaigns.

In bars, pubs, and restaurants, p-o-p materials consisted of pyramid-shaped table tents (reinforcing the brand's logo—a red triangle) that invited patrons to ask their server for a free scratch-off game card. The instant winners on this card were entitled to receive any one of a number of high-value Bass Ale premiums, including ceramic bottle openers, tote bags, coasters, key chains, suspenders and T-shirts, all with the familiar red triangle logo. The displays in package stores and supermarkets included case cards, bottle neckers, take-one pads, all featuring the sweepstakes and high value rebate offers. In the Spring campaign, the rebate was $8 per case, $2 on a six-pack; in the Fall, it was $6 and $1.50.

The grand prizes tied in with each promotional theme, inviting consumers to experience a bit of British life. The Spring Country Life promotion offered a five-star tour for two to London and the British countryside. The Fall campaign offered a trip to England and first-class tickets to one of Britain's legendary sports events: the Wimbledon Championships, the Royal Ascot, or the Henley Royal Regatta. Running along with the sporting theme sweepstakes was the Bass Ale Sports Trivia Challenge. This was a mail-in game with entry forms available in restaurants, pubs, bars, package stores and super-markets. Consumers who answered the trivia questions correctly won a Bass Ale bonus, a ceramic bottle opener.

The two-pronged campaign was declared an overwhelming success among consumers and distributors, providing Bass Ale with many positive results in addition to enhancement of the brand's image and an increase in awareness. The platform allowed Bass Ale to significantly increase its placement in new accounts all over the country, stimulating consumer traffic in numerous outlets.

Looking forward to 1989, Bass Ale plans to increase its promotional push and extend the British Life series with "Enjoy the British Pub Life" in the Spring, and "Enjoy the British Mystery Life" in the Fall.

A variety of promotional materials were prepared for the Country Life campaign, including a pyramidal table tent and a large counter card.

Building on the Lotto

CLIENT:
Kellogg Salada, Canada

AGENCY:
Gaylord Planned Promotions,
Rexdale, ON
(Duncan McLaren)

When people are interested in playing lotto, you get a head start on a promotion if you can offer them another chance to get into the game. That's what happened when Kellogg's cereals set up its own lottery across Canada, riding off the popularity of the highly successful interprovincial lottery schemes.

In essence, it was simplicity itself. The rules and instructions, plus an entry blank, were printed on the backs of a number of varieties of cereal. The consumer simply wrote in five numbers, from 1 to 50, in the five spaces on the entry form, sent it in with a proof of purchase, and waited for the lottery date.

On that date, five numbers were drawn. All tickets that had picked all five correctly were eligible for the grand prize drawing, with a prize of $150,000 in cash, or $1000 a month for the life of the winner, delivered through the purchase of an annuity. Those who picked four of the winning numbers were eligible for a drawing in which three Plymouth Challenger station wagons were awarded, and those who picked three right numbers were eligible for one of 100 Panasonic VCRs.

There was no national advertising in support of the program, leaving the entire support up to point-of-sale and other in-store material. This included shelf talkers and a highly-visible flash on the face of the participating brands, and the entire back of the package.

Miniature lottery key chains and novelties related to the theme added impact to the presentation of the promotion by the Kellogg sales force to the trade, and resulted in excellent support at the retail level. The receipt of over 300,000 entries generated by a non-advertised promotion indicated exceptional consumer involvement.

*The major promotional tool was the
package itself, which carried an
announcement on its face, and
devoted the entire back to the
promotion. It was supplemented by
a display header and a shelf talker,
but no newspaper advertising was
used.*

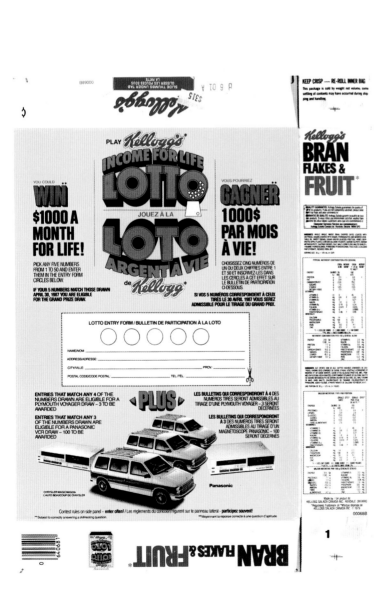

Not All Promotions are Mild

CLIENT:
Melcher's Canadian Whisky,
Adam's Spirits & Wines
International, Canada

AGENCY:
Gaylord Planned Promotions,
Rexdale, ON
(Duncan McLaren)

Rye whiskey is the largest selling category of distilled spirits in Canada, but across-the-board declines have been experienced recently. And a brand like Melcher's, which was acquired by Adam's four years ago, and had been given no advertising or promotional support in that period, was feeling the effects of the competition from some heavily advertised brands.

In Canada, consumption of rye whiskey is skewed to the 35+ group, with 70/30 percent split between male and female consumers. Consumer research indicated that the special blend of Melcher's, designed to provide a mild taste, was preferred by more women, with a 60/40 male-to-female split. Thus, it was quite clear that "mildness" was the obvious platform on which to base the brand's first in-store promotion.

A striking illustration, combined with the slogan "Born to Be Mild," was the central theme of the entire promotion. It was used on posters, backer cards, shelf-talkers, and neck tags. The program was limited to in-store materials only, with no print or other advertising. It ran for a period of one month only in each sales region.

With a budget of only $50,000, the average sales increase was 25 percent during the life of the promotion, and feedback was tremendous, from both the sales force and the trade. Originally run in 1987, it was repeated in 1988 with up-dated graphics and an increased budget. The second-year campaign included a free poster offer through in-store ad pads.

A striking photo formed the basis of the eye-catching stack header.

BORN TO BE MILD

**Aged 6 years
and blended to be
Very Mild.**

175

Black is Back and is Beautiful

CLIENT:
Brick Oven Bakeware/
Speko Products, Chicago
(Charles McClellan)

AGENCY:
Davidson Marketing Inc., Chicago
(Russell Blanchard, Dick Borgstrom,
Tom Baer, Virginia Van Cleve,
Chuck Shotwell)

People tend to think that a shiny set of cooking utensils is the sign of a good cook, but truly good cooks know that dark baking pans absorb heat better and produce better results. Brick Oven Black Steel Bakeware wanted to increase the awareness of this fact among the general public, and thus increase its sales volume.

Speko Products, the manufacturer of this line of bakeware, turned to Davidson Marketing to develop a promotional program that would reach both retailers and consumers. The product was ready to ride the wave of interest in black bakeware, based on the belief that it attracted and retained heat better—thus ensuring superior baking. But dramatic photography, sophisticated layout and upscale copy gave the promotion almost a high-fashion look, and distinguished it among both retailers and consumers from the routine appearance too often encountered in housewares promotion.

The trade had to be sold first, before consumer promotion could begin, so that the product would be available when consumers, attracted by the promotion and advertising, came in to satisfy their desire for the product. It started off with a stylish introductory brochure, using the theme "Black is Back," and four-color illustrations. Ads with color photography ran in the major trade publications and in key government food magazines. A broker sales incentive program tied in with the black theme with all-black prizes: blackjack in Las Vegas, black tie and tails in New York, and so on.

This started the product moving into the stores, and was soon followed by a campaign to get the consumer involved. Key element of the promotion was a cookbook, which presented unusual and interesting recipes of things to be baked in the Black Steel Bakeware. This was available to the consumer, free with purchase.

Special materials were produced for the point-of-sale, offering the purchaser a rebate by sending in a coupon with proof of purchase.

The entire campaign succeeded in giving this product line an excitement which emphasized its superb baking ability, and a glamour that, too frequently, had been lacking in the bakeware field.

The sales folder included the rules for the sales incentive contest.

BRICK OVEN BLACK STEEL BAKEWARE MEANS BUSINESS

BRICK OVEN
BLACK STEEL BAKEWARE
MEANS BUSINESS.

BLACK IS BACK
AND BRICK OVEN
MAKES IT BETTER
THAN EVER.

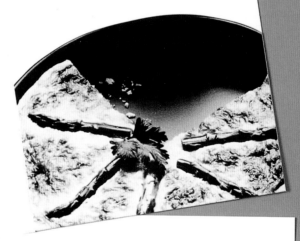

BE ONE OF THE
TOP FIVE TERRITORIES
IN SALES OVER QUOTA
AND CHOOSE
YOUR OWN REWARD

THE "BLACK IS BACK"
SALES CONTEST

THE BRICK OVEN™ BREAD WINNERS

Professional bakers will tell you—nothing bakes bread better than heavy black pans. That's why gourmet cooks who are into baking are turning to Brick Oven Black Steel pans for crustier, better-tasting breads.

CAKES, COOKIES AND SWEET TREATS BAKED THE BRICK OVEN™ WAY

Every little thing counts when baking scrumptious desserts. That's why serious bakers rely on Brick Oven bakeware for fail-proof results. Brick Oven Black Steel cookie sheets and dessert pans distribute heat evenly with no hot spots, to produce crusts that are flakier . . . textures that are moist and delicate. Consistent results time after time.

THE BRICK OVEN™ PIZZAS AND QUICHES

The secret to great-tasting pizza and quiches is the crust. And the secret to creating perfect golden brown crusts every time is built into all Brick Oven Black Steel pans. No other pans can match their exceptional baking properties.

BRICK OVEN™ GREAT BEGINNINGS

Brick Oven offers four-piece sets that make ideal starters or gifts. Each set features three of the most versatile baking items with an optional choice of one other piece. For your convenience, sets come packed in attractive display re-mailers.

IMPACTFUL PROMOTION TOOLS WILL HELP YOU MAKE BRICK OVEN™ BLACK STEEL BAKEWARE SELL ON SIGHT

When you use our promotion and merchandising programs, you'll clinch high-ticket (and high profit) sales of Brick Oven Bakeware. Each program is targeted to reinforce our powerful advertising selling message. Be sure you get your fair share of sales by using all of our promotion tools.

● Build traffic and sales with special in-store product demonstrations, available to qualified accounts.

● Prominently feature the Brick Oven Refund store display, along with plenty of Brick Oven products.

● Inquire about Brick Oven's co-op advertising allowance programs, available to qualified accounts. They can help you announce special promotions, pre-sell your customers, build additional store traffic and generate profitable extra business.

● Take advantage of our gourmet cookbook programs. We've adapted specially selected recipes for perfect results every time with Brick Oven Bakeware.

BRICK OVEN BLACK STEEL BAKEWARE MEANS BUSINESS

NATIONAL MAGAZINE ADVERTISING PRE-SELLS BRICK OVEN™ BLACK STEEL BAKEWARE TO YOUR CUSTOMERS

We're talking to gourmet cooks, people who are into entertaining, people who love to bake. The trendy ones. The style setters. The gift givers. And we're pre-selling all these people with upscale, full-page, full-color ads in major consumer magazines.

● We'll be telling the Brick Oven story in magazines like Gourmet, Bon Appetit, Better Homes & Gardens Holiday Cooking, Better Homes & Gardens Baking Ideas, Cuisine and Cooks.

● Millions of Americans who are serious about food and entertaining will see these ads during the peak baking (and selling) season.

● Stock Brick Oven Black Steel Bakeware in depth, display it, and be ready for sales when customers come in to your store, ready to buy.

Every purchaser of a piece of cookware was given a free copy of this high-style, attractive book of baking recipes.

The inserts prepared for the portfolio used a simple layout and more excellent photography.

An Emphasis
on What's Different

CLIENT:
Parliament Cigarettes, Philip
Morris USA, New York
(Marla Antonoff, Alex Aliksanyan)

AGENCY:
Backer, Speilvogel, Bates,
New York
(Ron Kraut, Barbara Shapiro)

There are about 256 brands of cigarettes currently marketed in the United States. That's a lot of competition, especially when the total market is declining at the rate of 2 percent annually. Parliament is especially strong in the Northeast, a region in which sales are declining even more rapidly than in the rest of the country. That makes this region an important one for this brand, and one in which it is worth expending considerable effort to maintain its consumer franchise and increase its share of the market.

The technique adopted in this program was to run a contest, calling upon buyers of Parliament to examine a full color spread in the regional editions of a group of major publications, including *Time, Newsweek, People, Playboy,* other major magazines, monthly supplements, and so on. Tying in with the major prize of a vacation a year for life, it was built around a "sketching" visual which had been used in Parliament advertising. The illustration was used on the left, and a mirror image of it on the right. But a number of changes—from 7 to 11 had been introduced into the right-hand image, and contestants were challenged to find them and mark them on the right-hand image.

The marked-up ad was to be sent, with two proofs of purchase, to Parliament. Each entrant who found all the differences received a free pack of Parliament Lights, and if he or she was not the only correct entrant, an invitation would be extended to a tie-breaking essay competition with the grand prize awarded to the essay that was judged the most unique, original description of the "Perfect Recess Columns" campaign. This was a special campaign shot.

Attention was called to the Perfect Puzzle competition by teaser newspaper ads directing readers to the magazine ads that had to be carefully studied to find the differences. Point-of-purchase displays reminded smokers of the contest when they came into the retail outlets. The use of a contest rather than a sweepstakes made it possible to require a purchase in order to enter, and provided a way to generate a product pull-through at retail.

This promotion generated a great deal of consumer interest and involvement. As a result, consumers were forced to become involved in Parliament's advertising in order to solve the puzzle. The promotion successfully accomplished both brand image and volume objectives.

Used in point-of-purchase displays, this card included a reproduction of the mirror image ad.

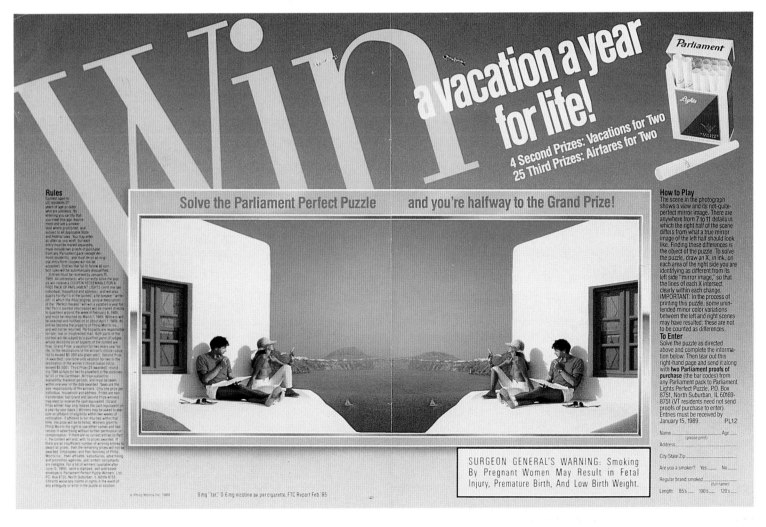

Idaho is a State of Quality

CLIENT:
J.R. Simplot Co., Boise, ID
(Heidi M. Glaysier)

AGENCY:
Sperling, Guy and Associates,
Boise

When MicroMagic, which produces a complete line of microwaveable sandwiches and milkshakes, recently added a new french fried potato to its line, it knew that it would have stiff competition, especially from the leading brand, Ore-Ida microwave french fries. But MicroMagic had a unique feature—it was the only product on the market that uses 100 percent Idaho potatoes.

To launch this new product successfully, MicroMagic knew that it had to educate consumers to the fact that it used nothing but Idaho potatoes in its french fries, so that it could gain acceptance, based on the public acceptance of the fact that Idaho potatoes have superior taste and quality.

The promotion had to have three targets: the consumer, the retailer, and the broker, and these three efforts had to support each other. All three were based on the state's slogan, "Famous Potatoes," which appeared on Idaho license plates, and on the public acceptance of Idaho and potato quality. Some 89 percent of all consumers associate quality potatoes with Idaho, and 69 percent believe a product with the Idaho seal is superior to one without. Moreover, MicroMagic is the only national brand which can make the claim of being 100 percent Idaho potatoes.

The promotion to brokers was built around extra payment for achieving an assigned case volume during the first 90 days of the program. In addition, exceptional performance could qualify a broker for special trips that utilized the heritage of the state, including rafting down a pristine river, or skiing in Sun Valley.

As a teaser, "Famous Potatoes" postcards were sent to buyers of frozen products for chains and individual stores. Trade ads appeared in the major publications in the field. Allowances were given on initial purchases of the french fries, but only if additional items from the microwaveable line were ordered at the same time. This was to encourage the idea that MicroMagic products could be used for a complete meal.

The most visible part of the promotion was directed at the consumer, starting with a full-page, free standing insert with a coupon. Special radio spots were used in key cities, as well as in-pack coupons and in-store sampling. Special "Taste Idaho" point-of-purchase was prepared to be set up near the frozen food case.

Month by month, as the promotion began to take effect, and as the state-by-state distribution grew, MicroMagic's percent of the dollar share of its category grew, and the figures indicate that by the time full national distribution will be achieved, it will be the dominant brand, due to a quality product and a quality promotion.

An in-pack leaflet carried a discount coupon, and encouraged regular buyers to try the new product.

Cards, 8''x6'', were used to call attention to in-store sampling offers.

Matching Ale and Hockey

CLIENT:
La Brasserie Molson, Montreal, Canada
(Nick Retson Bennet)

AGENCY:
Groupe Everest, Montreal
(Jean-Pierre Toupin)

For almost 50 years, Molson, one of Canada's leading brewers, had been sponsoring the broadcast of the Montreal Canadiens, first on radio and then on television. But it had never really utilized this connection as the basis for sales-building promotion. Just a few years ago, however, the picture began to change. The sale of wine was permitted in convenience stores, which meant that wine was now just as accessible as beer—and even less expensive! In addition, imported beers from the United States, as well as other parts of the world, began to cut into sales.

The brightest idea that came out of a Molson brainstorming session was to utilize, in a way that had never been done, the long-standing relationship between Molson and one of professional sports most winning teams—the Canadiens. The plan that emerged would build on this association and encourage purchase. It resulted in the first market share leap in many, many years!

The promotion was simple yet colorful. Under the cap of each bottle of Molson Export was printed one of 1,728 possible scores of a hockey game. If the numbers on one of your bottle caps matched the final score of a televised game, all you had to do was to phone a 1-976 number and register your entry. You did this by leaving your name, address, and telephone number, along with the validation code number from the cap. This was done automatically by a specially designed answering machine. It had to be specially-designed, since the average weekly response was more than 4,000.

Twenty-four hours after the close of the game, the answering machine stopped taking names, and five winners could be chosen by a computer. The prizes were, naturally enough, hockey related. They were just as simple to enjoy as the game itself, yet new and unique. They included box-seat tickets to a Canadiens home game; travel to an out-of-town game, including tickets, spending money, hotels; a private tour of the Montreal Forum, with ex-Canadiens acting as guides; dinner with ex-Canadien greats at the Forum's fine restaurant; and official Canadiens T-shirts.

The program had been planned for two hockey seasons, each lasting six months. The first year, 1987-88, the game was promoted with a 30-second television commercial and a 30-second radio spot, plus a public relations campaign. A key element, of course, was point-of-sale. Displays were installed in almost every retail outlet for Molson Export.

The next season, four 15-second television commercials were used, and a new 30-second radio spot, p-o-s displays, publicity, and recently, some print advertising. In addition, halfway through the season, a special effort was made to reach the "youth" market with a jingle and the back page of a major newspaper. This season, some of the caps were marked to offer T-shirts to instant winners.

Le Vrai Match was gaining a cult following. Clubs were formed among family and friends. Just like Bingo, people would sit in front of their television sets with their bottle caps spread out before them, eliminating scores as the games progressed. They were involved in every game, for six months. And they kept collecting bottle caps!

The promotion turned beer from a summertime favorite into a year-round drink. And, for the first time in years, Molson Export has succeeded in expanding its market share, and participation in the game is up by almost 10 percent.

A large poster at the point-of-sale explained how to enter the contest.

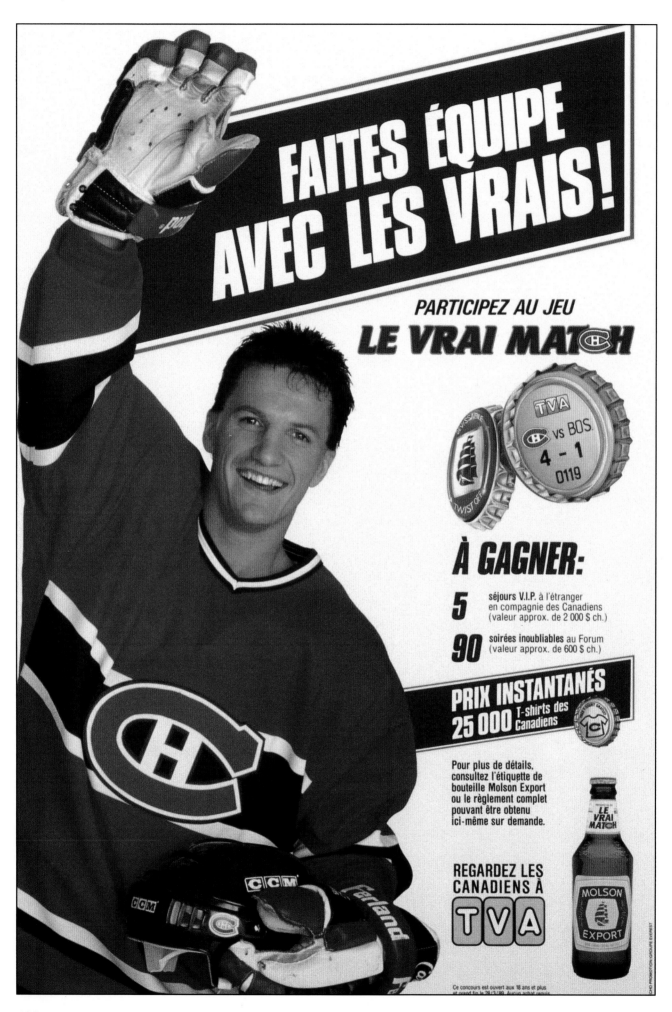

Material for the second year's
program included a game calendar
and a counter holder, a poster,
placemats, and a dangler.

Promotion in a Can

CLIENT:
Ketchum Public Relations,
Pittsburgh
(Jerry Thompson)
American Iron & Steel Institute,
Washington, DC
(David Jenes)

AGENCY:
Giltspur Exhibits/Pittsburgh
(Carl Shoemaker, Judi Baker-Neufeld)

Although steel maintains a dominant position in the food packaging market, it faces a stiff challenge from plastic materials in several food categories. Despite recent technological innovations and improvements in steelmaking, the market generally did not view steel as an exciting packaging material and a dominant market force. In one respect, at least, steel is more progressive than plastic, because its ability to be recycled, adequately addressed today's environmental concerns.

It was important to communicate this message to the food packaging industry, and Ketchum Public Relations—on behalf of the American Iron and Steel Institute, an organization representing eight major American steel manufacturers—suggested that AISI reinforce its position to this key target group by exhibiting at the International Exposition for Food Processors, that attracts representatives from food processing and packaging companies, including many buyers and specifiers of food packaging materials.

But just being there wouldn't be enough, especially when the space assigned to the client was only 600 square feet, and located at the very rear of the large exhibit hall, far from the primary traffic aisles. Giltspur/Pittsburgh, the trade show marketing company given the assignment, built an integrated marketing promotion around the theme "Steel—The Classic Package."

Giltspur's subsequent recommendations included a "classic hits" music theme, supported by a live show-site musical presentation called "American CanStand."

The pre-show promotion was a key factor in the integrated promotion strategy. A list of 618 key prospects was provided by show management, and each of these was sent a mailer designed to resemble a record album called "Steel Classics." The mailer included "the top tin hits as selected by major food processors, canners and can makers across the nation." The copy identified steel's performance benefits and invited the recipients to visit the exhibit to find out why steel is the classic package. A ticket to the live performances at the booth was included as a "call for action" to help AISE people identify key accounts on the show floor.

Both the invitation and the booth design reinforced the marketing messages of the AISI's ads and brochures, using photos and reiteration of copy points. The booth itself featured several 10-foot high steel cylinders with the messages "American CanStand" and "Steel— The Classic Package."

Immediately before the show opening, Giltspur conducted two training sessions for all the booth personnel. In addition to rehearsing the live marketing presentation, these sessions also reviewed AISI's objectives for the show and the interpersonal skills necessary to quickly identify and qualify key prospects. A reference training book with information about the live presentation was distributed to the booth staffers to provide ongoing support.

The live performance of American CanStand was performed hourly, with the entertainers dancing on three round platforms decorated to resemble tin cans. Their lively presentation promoted three critical marketing messages through songs entitled "Stand by Your Can," "R.E.C.Y.C.L.E.," and "Leader of the Pack." During the presentation, audience members were asked to complete lead-tracking forms that provided a company profile and identified immediate steel leads.

After each performance, members of the audience were invited to have their pictures taken on stage with the performers. The photos were enclosed in a silver and black "Steel Classics" folder to provide post-show reinforcement of the AISI marketing message.

The promotion didn't stop with the closing of the show. All leads were forwarded to each of the eight member companies sponsoring the exhibit, for their individual follow-up. In addition, a special thank-you package was developed to respond to prospect inquiries and to reiterate the key messages. The mailing included a specially designed box that contained a steel can, provided by one of the member steel companies. Inside was a steel measuring tape. The steel can was decorated with the "Steel Classics" message, designed to resemble a food packaging label. The thank-you note was produced as a miniature record album that included a die-cut disc listing the three songs from the trade show performance. The can label and thank-you note both featured steel's recycling story and a list of the eight AISI members. Nearly one-third of the target prospects responded to the pre-show mailing. The promotion and booth presentation generated 363 leads, of which more than 200 were rated "highly qualified." In addition, the efforts of Ketchum Public Relations and the media kit it prepared resulted in exceedingly good coverage in the trade press.

The pre-show invitation, sent to a selective list of key executives, played up the musical presentation, and included two tickets to the show.

The post-show package included a thank you folder, and a specially-labeled tin can, which held the ruler.

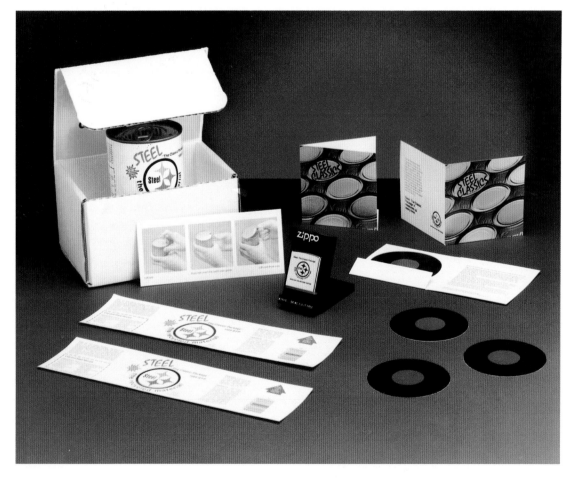

Other material developed for the show was a folder in which a photo of a visitor and a member of the cast was mounted, a staff training manual, an imprinted steel rule, and a lead card for use during the show.

Promotion for the Moment

CLIENT:
MasterCard International, New York
(Maureen Cronin)

AGENCY:
Giltspur Exhibits, Pittsburgh
(Philip J. Moore, Judi Baker-Neufeld)

MasterCard's slogan is "Master the Moment," around which its current advertising campaign is built. So when it was preparing to participate in the American Bankers Association National BankCard Conference, MasterCard wanted to integrate the slogan into the exhibit and related promotional activities.

The "Master the Moment" tagline was expanded for the exhibit to "Make Every Moment Count with MasterCard." This reinforced the interactive theme of the exhibit, and suggested to the audience that their association with MasterCard at the Conference would be an educational and enjoyable experience. The message was used in all pre-show mailers and invitations, as well as being incorporated into the exhibit design.

The pre-show promotion started with a special invitation sent to a list of 720 preregistered attendees furnished by show management. The unusual piece, only 4¼" square, opened out one panel at a time to display a floorplan of the exhibit, and invited the recipient to visit the booth. If his invitation were validated at the six primary brand name areas within the exhibit, he would qualify for a free gift, and was entered in a sweepstakes with a top prize of $5,000 in credit on the winner's MasterCard account.

To assure that traffic would continue through the last day of the show, traditionally a slow day, a ticket was included with the invitation. This invited recipients to come to the booth on the last day, and exchange the ticket for a baseball personally autographed in the booth by Cubs star Ernie Banks. In addition, attendees could enter a baseball survey, and qualify for a drawing for two tickets to the 1989 World Series.

A limited number of key customers and prospects were invited to meet Peter Hart, MasterCard's CEO, at the company's hospitality suite. The invitation featured the same stopwatch illustration used on the general invitation, giving additional image reinforcement.

When visitors came to the exhibit, they were asked if they had brought their invitation. If not, additional invitations were available, to encourage participation by all attendees. Each of the brand areas had a specific message to generate, along with a gift and/or a demonstration.

One of the two key focal points of the exhibit was a specially-designed Sports Trivia game, in which the visitor was asked one question about each of the sports of baseball, basketball, hockey and golf, to reflect MasterCard's major sports sponsorships. Those who answered all four questions correctly received a Cross Pen. Three questions answered correctly won a sleeve of golf balls. Two got you a "Master the Moment" T-shirt, and one an imprinted coffee mug.

The game was conducted by a professional master of ceremonies who included pertinent MasterCard information in his script. He also urged people to visit the other areas of the booth to get their cards validated, and to come back on Tuesday to meet Ernie Banks. It was a popular game, and many attendees returned several times to play. The area was crowded with people waiting to play, and booth staff were able to get acquainted and to talk to many customers and prospects.

The 21st Century promotion area was also heavily attended. This tied in with MasterCard's fourth quarter 1989 campaign. Attendees who completed a survey related to the campaign received a scratch-off card, about 10 percent of which awarded the recipient a Master the Moment wristwatch.

The ability to handle traffic flow and interact efficiently with target prospects was critical to the success of the promotion. Prior to the opening of the exhibit, all MasterCard exhibit personnel attended a 5-hour training session to learn effective tradeshow selling techniques. The course was personalized to the show, the exhibit, the promotion, and the

target audience. Basic boothmanship skills were reviewed along with pertinent information about MasterCard promotions and show objectives.

The company made every moment count for its friends by sponsoring a Monday evening dinner to hobnob with Wayne Rogers; a Sunday afternoon brunch on the verandah of the Opryland Hotel, at which guests could ascend in the Master-Card hot air balloon' and the "Meet Peter Hart" hospitality suite for key prospects.

A special folder duplicating the invitation graphics was used to fill requests for literature. It included a thank you letter from Pete Hart, as well as any literature requested at the show. Follow-up requests were handled by Giltspur Lead Management, which fulfilled requests within 24 hours of receipt of the lead.

Out of the 720 invitations sent out prior to the show, 465 prospects responded on the show floor. Not only was the 58 percent response outstanding, but it was 2½ times the original projection.

This elegant invitation unfolded to illustrate the six areas of the exhibit, and served as an entry blank for the sweepstakes.

A literature folder, used after the show, utilized the same graphics.

The understated booth furnished a good background to all the activity that was planned for it, while the black highlighted the transparencies.

The last day of the show was more popular than ever before, with baseball great, Ernie Banks, autographing baseballs for the visitor.

chapter FOUR

Clifford R. Medney
Director, Sales Promotion
A&W Brands Inc.

Displays are Critical

All great baseball teams have "a closer," a relief pitcher who ensures victory by stopping the competition from scoring late in the game. Similarly with consumer promotion, all great promotions deliver a closer, but unlike baseball, it isn't a relief pitcher but an in-store display. The display is the key player in stopping the competition from scoring late in the game. By catching consumer attention at the point of decision, the display is surely promotion's most valuable player.

The baseball analogy is inherently appropriate, because playing a great game for eight innings means nothing if you blow it in the ninth. Just like supporting a promotion with traffic-building elements, such as electronic media or FSI, means nothing if you lose the sale in the bottom of your ninth. According to the Point-of-Purchase Advertising Institute (POPAI), 66 percent of all purchase decisions are made in the store. Even more to the point, the war is on the floor, not on the shelves. If your competition is off-shelf, the game is over.

Why is getting on display so critical to sales success? Simply, a display says to consumers "Come look at me—I'm special this week —I'm a good deal; buy a lot of me." Granted, most displays can't talk, but if they could, that's what they would say.

It's this silent but real communication that consumers hear and respond to. And unlike advertising, the response to display promotions isn't in marketing terms but in sales terms. Words like volume, velocity and turn reflect the pay-off value of what the display delivers, This is validated in a research study by Information Resources Inc. (IRC) as featured in the March/April issue of *P-O-P Times*. The study was based on 789 brands in 166 categories. Its findings showed a sales increase in every category when a display accompanied a 10 percent unadvertised price discount. The weekly increases generated by the displays alone ranged from 17 percent to 231 percent, with an average gain of 85 percent. Because of the sales implications, it's easy to sell the field force on display promotions, but it is extremely limiting to view display events as being able to contribute to immediate sales alone. Effectively merchandised and presented displays can positively influence brand image, as well as, in the case of multi-brand displays, illustrate compatibility with other products (as in usage suggestions promotions). It's the broad sales and marketing impact that displays deliver that foster the phrase "The Jewel of the Aisle."

But like any sought-after jewel, the price can be high, considering most retailers view display space as real estate and charge for it accordingly. Many marketers and retailers have joined hands in signing Calendar Marketing Agreements, or CMA's. These ensure a marketer his share of displays and/or feature ads. The cost of CMA's differs with product category and geography. Generally speaking, they are not an incidental or incremental expense, but they do achieve a formatted and pragmatic display timetable, such as assuring 26 weeks of end aisle support in a year.

More traditional ways of securing display support take the form of trade deals, like performance allowances and case deals. In addition to monetary-based incentives, many product categories generate a display activity leveraging dealer loaders and other incentive activities, such as trade sweepstakes and contests. While many chain headquarters now formally prohibit their store managers from accepting or participating in promotional incentive activity, it is still a widely accepted practice that is often consummated in the parking lot.

While it almost always, in one way or another, comes down to a "pay to display," savvy marketers leverage other marketing elements to help persuade the trade to display their products. FSI, the delivery vehicle of choice, is also the leveraging device of choice. The trade loves FSI's because the lead time affords them the lead time to merchandise displays against the drop date. High levels or blasts of electronic media, especially tagged media, are alongside FSI's as an effective tactic to induce display support.

While these reflect delivery, the trade also responds enthusiastically to really dynamic consumer promotion offers. Developing a great consumer premium or sweepstakes that the trade can promote in their circulars and merchandise a display around, is an extremely effective approach to negotiating display space. The fact is the trade loves offers that their customers will love. However, most store managers know good from bad, so bring excitement or don't bring anything at all. The bottom line to leveraging media and consumer promotion is that alone it's usually not enough; but, add a thematically linked dealer loader, and it should get you the display.

Getting the display requires selling and haggling; maximizing it requires marketing and merchandising. Unique point-of-purchase materials and display loaders dramatically contribute to the display's attention-getting ability. Effectively merchandised displays reinforce the brand position which hopefully increases display velocity.

In addition, well-thought-out consumer promotions that beg for involvement are the cornerstones to paying off a display. Sure, most consumers look at the displayed feature price first, but a high perceived value self-liquidator or dream fantasy sweepstakes is sure to capture attention and possibly promote a sale. The reason for this is that consumers want added value and added opportunities. Promotions that deliver this make the displayed feature price work a lot harder. By following what I call the ABC's of promotion (Always Benefit the Consumer), you should instinctively deliver an appealing and involving display event.

In fact, displays spotlight your product, while highlighting its price. They tell consumers "I'm a player in a ballpark of bench-warmers." And with scanners keeping daily score, it tells the manager (store manager, that is) who is headed for "home." It's the "pile on the aisle," the "friend on the end" that's closing out the game every day!

Personalization Pays

CLIENT:
Culinar-Vachon
(Ms. I. Hudon)

AGENCY:
Promotion: Hains/Roberts,
Toronto
(T. Hains, C. Thouin, A. Stamml)
Design: TDH Communications, Toronto

AWARDS:
1989 CSPA Award of Excellence
(Finalist)

Vachon, a Canadian product, is in the highly competitive, impulse-directed snack food market. That's why mass displays have universally been used to stimulate impulse sales. According to POPAI, 79.8 percent of all snack food buying decisions are made in-store and are thus influenced by displays. Further analysis indicates that the highest buying groups of customers are a woman and child, followed closely by a family group.

In the past, Vachon products have offered the same promotional event to all accounts, ignoring the differences among supermarket chains. This promotion was based on the premise that if the company and its agency could offer a unique, personalized program to their major accounts, they could sell more product. This notion was tested in 1988 with three chains in Atlantic Canada.

In Sobeys' 100 stores, there would be a winner in each store who would receive ½ gallon of milk a week for one year. There were 83 stores in the IGA group, and the winner in each store would win a talking doll of Big Bird, the Sesame Street character. Customers in the 71 Save Easy stores could enter a drawing to win a summer fun raft, its size varying according to the store's display volume commitment.

Headers for mass display were developed for each of these offers, with the chain's logo featured on each. In addition to this, posters, ad pads and mats, and ballot boxes were prepared, using the appropriate theme. In the larger IGA stores, a costumed Big Bird was on hand during peak shopping hours to hand out coupon entries. All participants received the customary in-store draw allowance.

The response in the field was spectacular. In the Sobey stores, the regular movement of 21,000 cases went up during this promotion to 81,000. In the Save Easy stores, the increase was from 25,000 to 60,000. Finally, and most exciting, from almost no presence at all, at movement of only 1,000 cases, the IGA promotion boosted sales to 23,000!

The personalization resulted in exceptional in-store performance, and in 1989, the concept was extended into Ontario, and produced similar results. Other personalized concepts developed and introduced in 1989 maintained the momentum.

In IGA stores, there was a tie-in with the Sesame Street character, Big Bird. The winner would get a talking doll of the beloved character.

The header on this mass display offers a sweepstakes with a year's supply of milk as the prize.

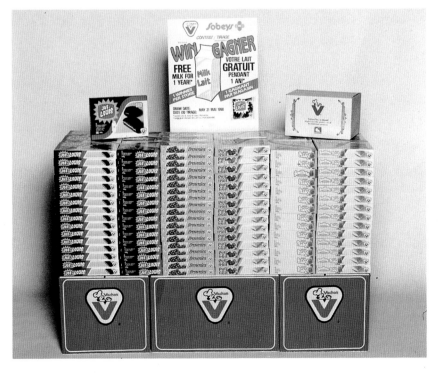

You Learn as you Promote

CLIENT:
Jerome Foods, Barron, WI

AGENCY:
Robert H. Meyers & Associates
Inc., Minneapolis
(Mark Bowers, Meda Carlson, Scott Webster)

Promotions are designed to meet objectives, usually generating an incremental increase in sales volume, but here's one whose secondary objective was to learn more about consumer usage and what appeals to consumers from a promotional standpoint.

The product was a line of fresh, boneless cuts of turkey, and the primary challenge was to establish this meat as a year round food, rather than its traditional position as a holiday feast. Jerome Foods Inc. is one of America's largest fully-integrated turkey growers, with over 60 years experience in turkey production and processing. In 1984 it introduced The Turkey Store, a line of fresh boneless turkey products, and in spite of heavy competition from Oscar Meyer, Jennie-O, and Hormel, the new line succeeded in getting a major share of its category.

In an effort to increase summer consumption of this product, Jerome and its sales promotion agency introduced The Turkey Store "Great on a Grill" promotion event. It was essentially a sweepstakes, with a grand prize of $10,000 in cash. Other prizes were 100 Weber Kettle Grills, 1,000 custom barbecue aprons, and 1,000 $5 coupon packets for the full line of Turkey Store products. Consumers simply sent in a proof-of-purchase along with the official entry blank. They received a $1 cash refund, and were automatically entered into the sweepstakes.

The promotion was introduced to the public with a full-page, free-standing insert, of which 18 million copies were circulated. When they came into the stores, other materials were there to attract their attention. These included full-sized free-standing Weber grill displays with a tear-off pad, tear-off pads for the meat case, hanging mobiles for use near the product, special packaging that promoted the sweepstakes, and free Turkey Store Cookout recipe books. All these materials were designed to generate excitement, suggest new summer usage, and boost sales.

But there was an opportunity to conduct market research, and Jerome and its agency went ahead with this side-line project. Four small market test areas were identified and used to see how changing the terms of the offer would change the consumer pull of the promotion. In these areas, a simple change was made to the FSI. Instead of the $1 mail-back refund, a 50¢ coupon was inserted, and a few minor changes were made in the copy. The idea was to see if an immediate reward, lower value coupon offer would outpull a delayed reward, but higher value cash refund offer. Consumers in these areas were automatically entered in the sweepstakes when they put their names and addresses on either the coupon or the rebate certificate.

Another technique, used in both the test and the national promotional event, was to ask consumers to check one of two boxes on the coupon or the refund certificate. This allowed the percentage of trial users attracted by the offer to be measured. A similar request was made on the packaging that was used to enter the sweepstakes only, without a refund.

A special kit was developed to merchandise the promotion to the retail trade. It included a brochure, reprints of the FSI, a list of newspapers in which it was to run, custom ad slick, Weber grill displays, tear-off pads, as well as product and promotion information. Special presentations, including a slide show, told the story of the promotion to brokers and key accounts. A Bonus Trade Performance Program was developed and implemented to draw stores into the event. Stores got case discounts and a free Sunbeam portable gas grill for adding previously-unordered items of the line, for using an ad, and for placing p-o-p material.

Record sales were generated by the promotion in all sales regions, averaging a 32 percent increase in core tray pack volume for the week after the FSI, compared to the four prior weeks. Trade acceptance was better than anticipated given the size of display. Jerome also recouped some previously lost distribution.

The tests brought out some interesting differences among groups of purchasers. First-time users comprised 27 percent of those who claimed the $1 cash refund, compared with only 15 percent for the 50¢ coupon. Thus, the higher value offer brought in about twice as many new users as did the lower one. While 40 percent of the respondents to the coupon did not indicate either way, only 12 percent of those who responded to the $1 refund failed to respond. Perhaps those who will wait for their reward are more concerned about fully cooperating.

Supporting elements of the promotion included floor displays, shelf talkers, counter cards, and premiums.

We've Got Your Summer Turkey Sales Made In The Shade!

Promotion Maintains Leadership

CLIENT:
Golden Valley Microwave Foods,
Minneapolis
(Jim Wattans)

AGENCY:
Robert H. Meyer & Associates
Inc., Minneapolis
(Keith McCracken, John Stewart,
Robert Weiner)

It's nice to be the first entrant in a new category, and it's even nicer when the category turns out to be a success. But success brings not only satisfaction, but also competition. That's the situation in which Golden Valley Microwave Products found itself after it was the first company to develop a microwaveable popcorn. As the category grew, competition grew, and there was a need for a substantial marketing plan designed to maintain and build sales volume and sustain market share.

Its "Act II" brand, shelf-stable microwave popcorn is its major brand and most popular consumer item. It dominates the vending and mass merchandise markets, as well as being a major player in drug stores, convenience stores, and video outlets. Each of these markets is different, and this promotion concentrated on the vending market, which was the first area of opportunity developed by GVMF. It has since become a major, multimillion portion of the company's activity.

The promotion developed by Golden Valley and its agency was directed at all segments of vending distribution, from the broker to the consumer, with special emphasis on vending machine operators, where a 50 percent sales increase was the target.

To get the promotion off to a good start, the company sponsored the first-ever national sales conference for GVMF brokers. This meeting, designed to enhance the marketing skills of the brokers, attracted 100 percent of the active brokers.

Distributors were reached by offering them off-invoice allowances, and their salesmen were eligible to enter a travel incentive program, themed to the consumer promotion and geared to increase case sales.

Both vendors and consumers were offered chances to enter separate "instant win" sweepstakes based on the movement of product. The campaign for vendors and their route salesmen was geared to increase the number of slots in the vending machines, thus increasing impact on consumers and increasing sales. This campaign was called "Cash in your Chips," a deliberate pun focusing on the need to reduce the amount of space given to chips. Every sale of product for a vending machine earned the salesman an entry, which was an instant win card that offered a chance to win a grand prize of a trip to Monte Carlo, and first prizes of trips to Las Vegas and Orlando. Second prizes were 1,000 silver dollars.

Consumers entered the game when they found a scratch-off entry form in each package of Act II popcorn they bought. There were four grand prizes of $5,000 each, 10 trips to Las Vegas or Orlando, and 20,000 prizes of one dollar each. Unusually high odds of winning were built into the prize structure to ensure consumer interest and encourage frequency of purchase.

The campaign was largely promoted at the point of sale, but there were special problems with developing a p-o-p piece, due to the nature and location of vending machines. A mini-poster was developed which was large enough to attract consumer attention, but not so large as to block other retail sales. Considerable field research was necessary to develop a size that would be widely acceptable. The material of this poster was specially designed to produce a static cling effect, and it was sized so that it could be affixed on the inside of the machine's glass door, thus ensuring that it would stay on the display for the period of the promotion.

GVMF had packed instant win game cards into a normal ten weeks' inventory, with the expectation that a 50 percent increase in sales might exhaust this inventory in six or seven weeks. Actually, sales quadrupled, and the inventory sold out in 17 days! As a result, the promotion was immediately repeated, with similar success for game 2.

ACT II®

Microwave Popcorn
Instant Gratification!

Robert H. Meyer & Associates, Inc.
4725 Highway 7 Minneapolis, Minn. 55416
Tel. (612) 920-5744

GOLDEN VALLEY
MICROWAVE
FOODS, INC.

Golden Valley Microwave Foods, Inc.
7450 Metro Blvd.
Edina, MN 55435

1-800-328-6286

© GVMF 1988

A-V-P-0001

The sell-in brochure outlined the total promotion, and was widely distributed to brokers, sales people, and vendors.

There was a scratch-off game card in every bag of popcorn.

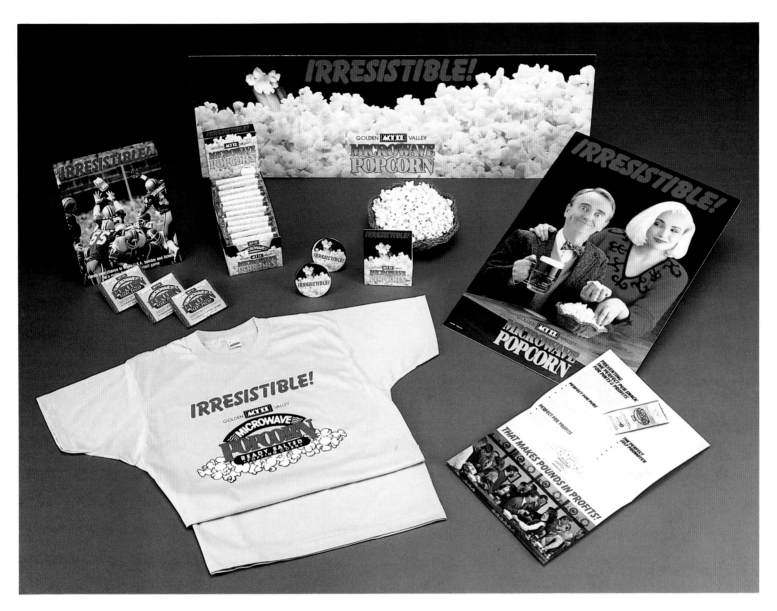

A broad variety of promotional materials, all carrying the slogan "Irresistible," was part of the program.

No Weeping
for this Willow

CLIENT:
Quaker Oats Co., Chicago
(Dan Strunk)

AGENCY:
U.S. Communications Inc.,
Minneapolis

AWARDS:
1989 CSPA Award of Excellence
(Finalist)

This was a major promotion for major products, supporting twelve products manufactured and distributed by the Quaker Oats Company. Utilized for products that ran the gamut from Cap'n Crunch to Rice-A-Roni, it had to have a broad appeal, attracting the attention of both children and their mothers. While Quaker runs promotions regularly in June and July, in previous years, June had been devoted to getting products into the retailers' hands, and July to moving them out to the customer. This year called for an integrated two-month continuous effort, leading to higher sales volumes for those products in the program.

The overall strategy involved leveraging the Lucasfilm name by tying in with "W-I-L-L-O-W", a major summer film whose all-family demographic appeal matched well to Quaker's audience. Quaker built on the timely awareness of the film to create excitement in both the sales force and the trade, as well as providing a hook for the consumer.

The prospect of success was exciting. After all, George Lucas, W-I-L-L-O-W's producer, had previously produced five of the eight top-grossing films of all time, films which had generated over $2.6 million in retail sales of licensed merchandise.

The first stage was to get the sales force enthusiastic about the promotion. This was done at 16 regional sales meetings, held simultaneously all over the country.

They were tied together with a video teleconference network, so that the word got out directly from the top, and indicated, by its very scope, the importance management put on this promotion.

Everything was done to whip up excitement. At each meeting, there were mock-ups of all point-of-purchase displays that would be used during the promotion, as well as samples of all other sales support materials, including W-I-L-L-O-W T-shirts and Lucasfilm hats for all those attending the meeting. Movie one-sheet posters were used to decorate the meeting rooms.

A full program was developed for the sales force to use in presenting the promotion to the trade, as well as materials to be used by the stores to reach their publics. First among this was a presentation box which held a tape of the sales video, an MGM full-color book about the film, and a sales brochure which told the story of the movie, the tie-in, and the promotion.

To encourage the build-up of inventory for this two-month promotion, a number of offers were scaled to case sales, including point-of-sale displays, special trade gifts and dealer loaders, all identified as "W-I-L-L-O-W." Ad slicks and in-ad coupons were made available, and there were aggressive trade deals and merchandising allowances for

merchandising performance. In selected markets, buyers and key managers were invited to special showings of the film, and dinners were held for key accounts where the program was introduced.

The promotion was announced to the public in a three-page free-standing insert spread distributed June 10. Consumers were offered a coupon which entitled them to free milk when they purchased any two of the participating cereals. In addition, there was a mail-in certificate for a free W-I-L-L-O-W bowl and spoon, which they could get by sending in proofs-of-purchase from two different cereals. The promotion was supported in the store by a variety of point-of-purchase displays, which included a motorized end-aisle display in 3-D, which held a tear-off pad. A smaller version of this was flat and did not use a motor, and a display banner was also made available.

In July, a 10-page free-standing insert was used to communicate corporate and individual brand W-I-L-L-O-W offers. On a corporate basis, the consumer could get a toy with proofs from any three of the participating products, and a cap with five. Cap'n Crunch had a cents-off coupon in this FSI, and announced that its packs would contain one of three premiums:

magic cards, a disappearing coin slide, or a magic window. This in-pack offer was announced on the front flag and the back panel of 16 million packages, and was supported by six weeks national TV advertising.

Oh!'s used the FSI to deliver high value coupons, and to announce its on-pack offer of a storybook and tape, as well as a self-liquidating on-pack offer for other Lucasfilm movie videos. This offer appeared on 5 million packages.

The promotion reached the highest display levels in Quaker history, reaching 63 percent nationally, with some markets going as high as 80 percent penetration. Sales volumes exceeded all the objectives that had been defined at the beginning of the promotion, and the sales excitement was so great that both trade executives, and the company's sales force asked that the promotion be repeated the next year.

The sell-in material was elaborate, including a videotape that captured the excitement of the film.

Free-standing inserts were used to attract consumers, with the single page example covering all the cooperating brands, while the spread concentrated on the dry cereals.

A custom banner was available to tie two end-aisle displays into a single massive unit.

An assortment of premiums could be obtained both as in-packs and by sending in proofs of purchase.

The Munsters at Halloween

CLIENT:
A&W Brands, White Plains, NY
(Cliff Medney)

AGENCY:
Comart-KLP, New York
(Stephen H. Stenstrom)

AWARDS:
1989 CSPA Award of Excellence
(Best of Category)

While A&W Root Beer and Cream Soda are leaders in their particular flavor categories, they are relatively small compared to Coke, Pepsi, 7-Up and Dr. Pepper. Yet they must compete with the big boys for display and feature ad support, and for sales time and attention from A&W's local bottlers, many of which handle one or more of the competitive brands. Yet displays are critical to gaining incremental consumer sales. Halloween is, of course, the primary merchandising theme during October, and retailers are looking for materials that help merchandise Halloween throughout their stores.

This promotion was designed to gain October displays of both A&W flavors in 20,000 grocery stores. If you can get a display built around attention-getting point-of-purchase material, you are certain to build impulse consumer sales. A&W expected this promotion to increase sales by 10 percent to 15 percent.

A&W tends to be a family product and therefore leads itself to a promotional theme that relates to a family holiday such as Halloween. For this promotion, A&W tied in with a well-known and popular family of Halloween characters—the Munsters. This television series ran from 1964 to 1968, and has been in syndication ever since. In September 1988, the Munsters were brought back and updated in a new series called "The Munsters Today." This revival provided an excellent tie-in opportunity for A&W.

A consumer sweepstakes was the center of the promotion. The Grand Prize was a trip to Hollywood, during which the winners would meet the Munsters. Eight such prizes would be awarded, one in each A&W sales region. Other prizes included Munster Revenge videos and Munster T-shirts. Point-of-sale materials featured the very recognizable Munsters, holding mugs and glasses of A&W. The key piece was a unique 45" long dimensional "A&W Munster Mobile" designed to hang over the A&W floor display.

To supplement the sweepstakes offer, an A&W plastic trick-or-treat bag was made available as a near-pack "free with purchase" offer. The bag featured the Munsters, as well as A&W Halloween safety tips. To help retailers decorate their stores during this holiday season, A&W offered inflatable and honeycomb pumpkins and A&W honeycomb ghosts. These were offered as store-wide decorative materials.

To sell-in the promotion to both bottlers and the trade, a specially-produced video tape was produced. Ad slicks were offered retailers for dropping into their regular ads, promoting either the sweepstakes or the trick-or-treat bag.

The promotion, with its variety of materials offered to retailers, resulted in an estimated 35,000 displays, each of which resulted in an important off-the-shelf display. According to the October/November Nielsen report, A&W's market share reached an all-time high! Most importantly, bottler case sales for October 1988 were 20 percent larger than October 1987, in spite of the fact that there had been a special Halloween promotion in the earlier year!

The "Munster Mobile," 45" long, was designed to hang over the floor display to call attention to it from anywhere in the store.

Tying in with a Film

CLIENT:

Kraft Inc., Chicago

(Ron Toyama)

AGENCY:

U.S. Communications Corp.,
Minneapolis

(G.A. Corky Hall)

In recent years, the overall cheese category has been relatively flat, growing at less than 3 percent per year, resulting in increasing price competition to build volume. Since most of Kraft's competitors are private label and regional brands, they are often at a price disadvantage at retail. Therefore, a significant part of marketing efforts is devoted toward gaining price reductions at the shelf. This approach, however, has turned out to be very costly, and Kraft has shifted its focus toward providing value-added incentives to purchases.

Studies have shown that significant volume increases can be attributed to retailer displays and feature ads. While many of the Kraft cheeses must be refrigerated, and thus not easily displayed, end cap placements and feature ads with price reductions can be effective in generating incremental volume. But, of course, space in retailers' dairy cases is limited.

One of Kraft's traditional promotions, an annual event, is called Cheesefest, and takes place during National Dairy Month in June. By combining the resources of its major cheese brands, Kraft hoped to gain trade support for massive displays and dominant feature ads. But Cheesefest had been only moderately successful in building trade support, and becoming increasingly expensive, with little or no incremental displays. It became clear that a different direction was called for.

In a year that would see both the Presidential conventions and the Olympic Games competing for the public attention, with projected increases in free-standing inserts and coupons vying for the consumer's eye, it would take something special to break through. Kraft decided to capitalize on the awareness, interest, and appeal of a major motion picture release, "W·I·L·L·O·W," to generate excitement in the marketplace.

The promotion was built around a number of unique and exclusive premiums which allowed the consumer to share in the adventure of W·I·L·L·O·W. These included a set of four placemats, a collector's series of three posters, plus a free movie poster which was available in participating retailers. In addition, Velveeta carried in-pack stickers.

The film was to be released on May 20, 1988, with a heavy advertising schedule. On May 22, five Kraft Cheesefest brands ran a two-page FSI which included a mail-offer for the free set of four W·I·L·L·O·W

placemats. In addition to the ad, the point-of-purchase materials included display banners, price cards, dairy case header cards, and tear pads. In addition, a specially designed castle display was created as a three-dimensional corrugated replica of the castle shown in the movie. This was used on large free-standing cheese displays during the Cheesefest promotion.

In specially selected stores, more than 5500 of them, Kraft hired in-store demonstrators to distribute a specially-designed coupon booklet which featured a mail-in offer for the collector poster series. These demonstrators also set up near-pack displays of the movie poster, each display holding 200 posters, one to be given away free with the purchase of any two Kraft cheese products. In markets not covered by demonstrators, a two-page FSI offered a coupon booklet specially designed by ACTNOW.

This program not only achieved increased levels of trade merchandising support, it did so while spending significantly fewer dollars than the prior year. Promotion spending for this, excluding normal deals, was 25 percent under the 1987 comparable figure. In total, over two million free posters were distributed in 12,000 stores nationwide, and approximately 70,000 sets of placemats were sent out by the end of the promotion.

To create excitement about the film, its story was told in a folder. In many areas, special previews of the film were run for retailers.

The first free-standing insert stressed the offer of the set of four placements.

A striking replica of the castle from the film added excitement to mass displays.

The set of three posters was the
basis of a promotion within a
promotion.

A variety of promotion pieces were
used to add color to the displays.

Let's Make Lunchtime, Funtime

CLIENT:
Campbell Soup Co., Camden, NJ
(Terrance Atkins)

AGENCY:
QLM Associates, Princeton, NJ
(Tony Mitchell)

AWARDS:
1989 Spire Award, Food
Category, American Marketing
Association

Campbell's, the leader in the soup category, has long established a positive image in the minds of consumers as a trusted provider of wholesome food. It has strong ties to American family life. The familiar Campbell's Kids represent the company and its products.

Not surprisingly, users of Campbell's Soup reflect the family imagery projected by the company. Nearly half of soup buyers have at least one child. Children under 18 have soup for lunch at least once every two weeks. And 39 percent of all children between 6 and 17 go home for lunch. Campbell's Soup has always had a position of being a soup that tastes great and is part of a healthy, hot, satisfying lunch. The peak kids' soup selling season begins during the Back to School season.

Binney and Smith Inc., the manufacturer of Crayola products, is also a leader in its category. The familiar red and white of Campbell's Soup and the green and orange of Crayola share the same consumer perception of trusted high quality products for children, so a joint promotion was a natural.

The national joint effort tied the two slogans—Campbell's "the soup kids love to eat" and Crayola's "the crayons and paints kid love to play with"—together in a back-to-school promotion called "Lunchtime is Funtime." This joint promotion was launched via Mailbox Values/Direct Mail Program which distributed 46 million copies of a promotional offer. Parents could mail in for a Crayola washable color paint set, free with ten proofs of purchase of Campbell Soup. They could also pick up a trial pack of Crayola crayons when they bought any two Campbell's Kids' Soups. A large display kit contained the near-packs of the free Crayola crayon sample packs and the mail-in certificates for the free paint set.

Campbell's expanded its promotion by offering the trade an in-store consumer coloring contest called "Color for Fun." In-store point-of-sale announced the contest and directed consumers to tear pads entry sheets. They took them home for their children to enter, and brought them back and placed them in the Campbell entry box at the store. Store management selected one winner in the 1 to 6 age category, and another in the 7 to 14 category, and awarded each a Crayola product which was presented to the winner.

The two prize winners from each store were forwarded to Campbell for final judging. Five Apple II-C computers were awarded to the grand prize winners.

The program was sold in using a special kit for the sales staff. It was a trade brochure in coloring book form, a custom lunchbox with crayons, a thermal bottle, and Campbell's soups. Once a store agreed to participate, it was sent a merchandising kit to assist in creating off-shelf displays. This contained the first place prizes to be awarded to local winners, plus posters, banners, case cards, ad slicks, and a separate carton for the near-pack samples of Crayola.

Campbell's regional marketing and sales groups were able to supplement the national programs with their own separate funds. For example, black-and-white coloring books, illustrated with the Campbell's kids and customized with the grocery chain's logo, were offered in the stores' own ads, free to consumers with any Campbell's Kids soup purchase.

The "Back to School" program was extremely well-received by both Campbell's sales force and the trade. It created much more trade enthusiasm for developing displays and in-store promotion overlays than Campbell's had hoped for. It netted over 6500 end-aisle displays, and an incremental volume increase of 6.2 percent over the previous year, a significant jump in a mature business.

The elements of the promotion—kids, coloring, and soup—were clear from the moment the buyer opened the sell-in brochure.

Other presentation pieces used recognizable art that told the story of the special promotion.

A die-cut header promoted the near-pack premium of two crayons with a purchase of two cans of soup.

Banners, posters, and stack headers were all available to spread the word.

Tell It with the Marines

CLIENT:
The Mennen Company,
Morristown, NJ

AGENCY:
Not Available

AWARDS:
1989 CSPA Award of Excellence
(Finalist)

The Mennen Company was facing a gloomy situation in the last quarter of 1988. While the year had started out well, growth had slowed as the year went on. Part of the reason was that the previous year's promotion had not left a float of coupons in consumers' hands to help drive sales in 1988. In addition, the company's competitors in the categories where they overlapped had presented strong programs.

That made the last quarter a key one for Mennen. In order to reach critical mass and its accompanying impact on the market, it would be essential to move product to floor displays. But the last quarter of the year is a difficult one for manufacturers of health and beauty aids products. This is a strong sales period, with its exciting holidays, and stores have a bias against using their precious floor space for health and beauty aids products. To overcome this, the program to be created had to be one which would gain trade support for displays and ad features, breaking through the seasonal promotion clutter.

The solution was to give massive support to the United States Marine Corps Toys for Tots program. This was a timely, cause-related theme, instantly recognizable to both consumers and to the trade, and accepted as a worthwhile goal by everyone. Mennen concentrated on getting its dealers to act as official collection centers, furnishing large, decorated bins to receive donations of toys from consumers. More than 5,000 of these bins were installed during the campaign.

Mennen worked closely with the Marines in placing and promoting the program. The commanding officer of the Marine Reserve prepared a video presentation that explains the history of the Toys for

Tots program, and asks for the support of the trade for the Mennen program. In addition, working with 250 Marine Corps Reserve sites around the country, Marines were invited to accompany Mennen sales personnel to explain the total program to chain buyers and store managers.

A two-page spread, free-standing insert ran nationally on November 6, explaining the program and included high value coupons on all of Mennen's participating brands. The graphics on this ad were related to those on merchandising elements, and supplied quick recognition and acceptance at the point-of-sale. Window banners identifying the store as an official collection center added to the impact of the program. In addition to the toys contributed by consumers (who deposited them in the in-store collection boxes), Mennen contributed $200,000 worth of toys, working with Hasbro/Playskool to get the highest retail value, and thus the greatest number of toys within the budget.

One of the interesting developments of the program was the way in which it was extended by individual accounts all over the country. In the Drug Emporium in Philadelphia, for example, in addition to major end-aisle displays, there were in-store appearances by the Philadelphia Eagles' Cheerleaders, accompanied by Marines. The store offered $5 coupons on future Emporium purchases to any customer whose toy donation had a value of $15 or more. This tie-in led to the placement of collection bins at the December 4 game between the Eagles and the Redskins. Eighty bins of toys were collected at Veterans Stadium.

The Atlanta division of Krogers tied the Toys for Tots program into its own Santa Claus promotion. Santa flew by helicopter to Kroger stores to meet the kids, and the toy bins were there for toy donations. Newspaper and in-store displays promoted the dual event. In Indianapolis, the Kroger chain dedicated one-half a page of its weekly ad to announce its support and to designate its stores as official collection centers.

The effect of the promotion on sales was evident. In one region, 50 percent of all drug, food, and mass merchandiser chains participated in the program with bins or displays. And 75 percent participated with ad features, up from 58 percent participation the previous year.

The header for a mass display used the logo and an eye-catching photo of Marines and a kid.

The Route to Success

CLIENT:
Schweppes USA, Cadbury
Beverages, Stamford, CT
(Kristen Miller)

AGENCY:
Promotional Innovations,
Stamford, CT
(Jim Zembruski)

Carbonated beverages seem like national products, and while most brands are advertised and distributed nationally, all production and distribution is local. The product you buy at your supermarket is produced and sold locally, with each area being serviced by an independent bottler. And even within a particular bottler's territory, the key man is the route man, who knows his customers and is responsible for building displays in-store to move product and communicate the promotional message. That's why he is an important person.

To reach this man, Promotional Innovations developed a contest for Schweppes USA, which was designed to motivate the route man to achieve the objectives considered desirable by the bottler for whom he worked.

Called "Quest for the Best," the incentive ran for the four summer months, from May through August of 1988. The Schweppes field representative sat down with each of the bottlers he visited to set a specific, measurable objective for each of the four months. These were key local goals—display placement, feature ads, distribution, shelf placement, and so on.

These objectives were entered on that month's poster, which listed a group of related prizes which the route men could win. May was fishing month, and the prize was the winner's choice of a tackle box, a rod and reel, a pair of waders, a fisherman's vest, or a Coleman cooler. Each month had a different theme, and a related group of prizes.

The poster, with the local objectives entered on it, was put up where all the drivers could see it. There was room for the winners to be listed. Each routeman who attained the month's objective could select one of that month's prizes. In addition, he and the bottler would be entered in a drawing for a $2,500 cash prize.

Allowing the bottler to set his own goals for each of the four months gave great flexibility to the promotion, as well as a sense of participation, and assured that the promotion would have local support. It generated increased route sales interest.

Each of the four posters, one for each month, illustrated the prizes that could be selected, had space for the bottler to write in the local objectives, and for the winners' names to be posted as they qualified.

A simple four-color folder was used to outline the promotion to bottlers.

A Bargain Price
without a Bargain Image

CLIENT:
Schieffelin & Somerset

AGENCY:
Focus Marketing, Norwalk, CT

Schieffelin & Somerset imports and distributes a premium selection of spirits and wines, marketed under a number of respected brands, including Johnnie Walker, Tanqueray, Hennessey, Moet, and Ruffino. But each of these must compete for retailer display space against companies with much greater sales power. The assignment given to Focus Marketing was to find a way to harness the combined power of the client's brands.

Three objectives were defined at the start of the project. The first was to create a display concept which could win major space for an extended period. The second was to solicit retailer price-featuring without impairing the premium image of S&S brands, and finally, to develop a flexible concept that would appeal to varying needs of retailers.

The solution to this problem was to develop a display concept under the theme "Duty Free Shop." This would offer consumers the chance to obtain fine premiums manufactured in the countries from which the imported brands came, and to do it at a cost that matched duty-free prices. The premiums were listed in a brochure that romanced each brand and its country of origin along with the premiums being offered. Consumers picked up the catalog at the point-of-sale, and placed their orders directly.

The displays offered to the retailers took a variety of forms. There were cards to mount on bins, as well as counter cards and case cards which could be used with any of the brands. Mobiles, shelf talkers, and so on, were made available.

The timing of the promotion was the real reason for its success. It was scheduled to run immediately after the Christmas holidays. At this time, there is not only a lull in competitive programming, but there is also a need for the retailer to deplete left-over holiday inventory. The flexible duty-free shop idea permitted each retailer to promote those brands that needed the most attention.

There was overwhelming trade response to the idea, and the success it achieved in its initial year has earned the concept a regular place on S&S's promotional schedule.

The counter top display held a supply of catalogs for the consumer, and the store manager could include any of the brands he wished to push as part of the display.

The introductory brochure for retailers had its quiet grey background accented with a colorful suggestion of national flags.

TAKE-ONE COUNTER CARD

chapter FIVE

Rae Ann Hoffman
New York World Trade Center

The Key to Building Traffic

Traffic-building promotions are designed to draw people to specific locations. They are used by individual stores, chains, malls, restaurants, car dealers, gas stations, ballparks, arenas, and similar entities. The underlying presumption is that attracting a sizable increase in traffic will result in incremental sales increases for the sponsors, store and promoter.

How do we motivate people to drive the extra mile, take the extra time, consider patronizing a different store or brand or dealer? The following is a summary of standard techniques used in traffic building promotions:

- I'll get something useful or valuable or fun for free. (Free premium)
- I might win something (Sweepstakes, instant win)
- I may already have won something, but I have to go "there" to find out what. (Match and win)
- I'll get a big discount or savings if I go now. (Off-price retailing; close-outside)
- I'll get special treatment. (Personal shopping service)
- I'll enjoy a special or unusual experience. (Special events marketing)
- Something is happening which my kids will enjoy. (Entertainment/special events)
- I'd like to help that charity or help that cause. (Charity tie-in or donation by sponsor)

Here are some examples of traffic-building promotions, accompanied by some of my personal comments:

FREE PREMIUMS
- Test drive the new Eagle Premier and get 3 golf balls, free. (*This kind of traffic-building promotion can overwhelm a dealer, but in this case, the advertising was limited to the golf magazines and cable TV golf tournaments, a high income group.*)
- Get a glass with NFL team logo, free with fill-up of Mobil premium. (*This is not strictly a traffic-building promotion because it is tied to a sale. But there are enough NFL football fans for this kind of promotion to create traffic if it's well advertised.*)
- The first 10,000 fans into the stadium get a free team cap (or jacket, or bat, etc.). (*These special bat day promotions always draw extra traffic.*)
- Visit a Shell station and buy these special Cruisin' Classics tapes for only $1.99. No purchase necessary. (*Self-liquidating premiums, in general, will not draw traffic as well as free premiums, but in this case the custom-made nature of the tapes and the excellent value, plus heavy advertising, resulted in over 5 million tapes being sold.*)

SWEEPSTAKES (*Instant Win, Match and Win, Collect and Win*)
- Bring your Sears credit card into Sears and match one of the numbers on the display, and win $5,000. New winners posted each week. (*Since you have to go to the store to find out if you won, this is traffic-building. Trade reports suggest it was not very successful, perhaps because the prize was so small.*)
- Buy a box of Tide. Inside every box is the key to a Chevrolet. Take the key to your Chevy dealer and try the key in the special ignition. If the key works, you win a new Chevy. (*This kind of promotion draws a lot of traffic to Chevy dealers but also creates problems, since the large majority of visitors are not in the market for a car, and the salesmen waste a lot of time. The issue of qualified traffic is discussed further near the end of this introduction.*)
- Visit McDonald's and collect game pieces for Monopoly. No purchase necessary. Millions of instant winners. Collect the sets and win big prizes. (*Combining instant win with collect and win increases the frequency of visits as well as traffic. This kind of promotion works best for high frequency visits and purchases such as fast food and gasoline stations.*)

SPECIAL SAVINGS/DISCOUNTS

- This month only, save $1,500 on a new Pontiac. (*Automotive rebates are legendary. For the long term, these create a mind set that people won't buy unless there is a special deal. These are not strictly traffic-building devices since they are tied to purchase. But they often get more people to come in for a look.*)
- Your Mitsubishi dealer has a special Three Diamond credit card waiting for you. If you qualify, you can buy a large screen Mitsubishi TV before Super Bowl Sunday and pay no interest for 12 months. (*Credit is increasingly being used as a lever for big ticket purchases, including cars.*)
- Loss leaders are used by many types of retailers, including supermarkets to draw traffic. For expensive items, such as appliances, TVs, etc., there is often a caveat of "While supplies last."

SPECIAL TREATMENT

- You are cordially invited to a close-door, after-hours sale at Bloomingdales. Our full complement of sales staff will be on hand to give you special attention. Since this sale is limited to only our best customers, you must bring this invitation with you. (*People like to feel special, and be accorded special treatment. In general, these kinds of sales are very successful.*)

SPECIAL EXPERIENCE

- Meet Mayor Ed Koch who will autograph his book.
- Meet Larry Bird who will autograph basketballs.
- Come to Gallagher's restaurant and meet Phil Simms while we broadcast a live show.
- Come to XYZ shopping mall and see Jimmy Connors play Andre Agassi on a special court in the parking lot. All the tennis gear in the mall is on sale. (*Celebrities are used in a variety of ways to draw traffic.*)
- The Beach Boys will give a concert in the mall.
- A well-known radio or TV show will be broadcast live from our shopping mall.

SPECIAL EXPERIENCE FOR KIDS

- Meet Santa Claus.
- Balloon rides in the parking lot.
- A whole carnival in the parking lot.
- Disney or Sesame Street characters in the store.
- A kid's TV show broadcast live from the mall.

CHARITY TIE-INS

- For everyone who comes into the store we will donate x amount of dollars to the March of Dimes.
- Every purchase of gasoline will result in a donation to the Little League equipment fund. (*This reflects a very local flavor, which is frequently more successful in motivating local residents than using big national charities as the tie-in.*)

In considering whether to use a traffic-building promotion, there are a few key issues to address from a strategic standpoint.
- Will I sell enough additional merchandise just by drawing traffic?
- Do I sell an expensive "considered" purchase rather than an impulse item?
- Do I want only qualified traffic?
- Are there potential long-term benefits?

The "Win a Chevy" sweepstakes is an interesting example. Hordes of people in the showroom make it difficult for salesmen to find the real shoppers/buyers. Many dealers have a problem with this. On the other hand, if there is a new car that needs exposure, as the Chevy Lumina did, some of the tire kickers may return in six months and buy the car. This requires a long term marketing perspective.

Sophisticated database marketing techniques make it possible for stores and dealers to focus on high potential qualified traffic, especially those stores which have their own credit cards. On the other hand, most malls/department stores/discount stores, and frequent visit locations such as fast food restaurants and gas stations, will benefit financially from traffic-building activities.

A Gingerbread House
Held the Solution

CLIENT:
Robin Hood Multifoods,
Willowdale, ON
(Craig Miller, Peter Reid, Jill Snyder)

AGENCY:
Promotion Solutions Group,
Toronto
(Dermot O'Brien, Leslee Vivian, Bonnie
Journeau, Joan Leathwood, Ala D. Hiltz,
Tim Sampson, Larry Mogelonsky)

AWARDS:
1989 CSPA Award of Excellence
(Best of Category)
Baking Festival Event for 1989

Robin Hood Multifoods is a major Canadian manufacturer of baking ingredients and mixes, and its flour leads the Canadian market with a 50 percent market share. Every year, Robin Hood sponsors a Fall multi-brand merchandising event with other major participants to encourage displays of baking products during the key 8-week baking season. But so do other suppliers of baking products, and one well-recognized promotion comes just before the period considered Robin Hood's. The latter has been considered the stronger, but it must maintain this leadership, or the earlier displays might very well be left standing longer, and cut into the time of the Robin Hood promotion.

The winner depends on a number of factors, including the prominence of the companies which become Robin Hood's partners, and the ability of the display to attract attention. This year a new appeal was added: the special objective of involving children, who are really the future in baking, into the promotion and into baking.

The promotion was built around three different displays, all ginger-bread houses. These differed essentially in size, one being 10' x 20', the second 10' x 10' (both of these free-standing) and the third a smaller end aisle unit. All were complete baking centers, with the space shared with Procter & Gamble's Crisco; General Foods' Baker's Chocolate; E.D. Smith Pie Filling; Borden's Eagle Brand; ReaLemon; Sun Maid Raisins; as well as Robin Hood Flour.

Key element in the display was a 32-page cookbook incorporating recipes from all participating partners, with the addition of Sunbeam Appliances. For the first time, this year's booklet contained a special children's section, with an easy to bake cookie recipe. It also offered to send a free personalized "Official Baker" certificate to any child who requested it. Nearly 3 million of these booklets were distributed as inserts in *Homemaker's* and *Canadian Living* magazines, and 1.4 million were distributed at the displays, using a holder mounted on each.

Stores were offered an opportunity to gain additional mileage from the promotion by holding its own sweepstakes with the gingerbread house from the display as a prize. A ballot box was built into the display for this purpose. If the store did not want to participate in this local event, a sticker was provided to cover the in-store draw information.

All the point-of-purchase materials were used, totalling 750 of the 10'x 20' units; 1200 of the 10'x 10' units; and 3,000 end aisle displays. The Children's Baking Section was an incredible success. 500 responses were expected; 5,000 were actually received. Robin Hood Flour volume was up 12 percent compared with the preceding year, and the other participants achieved their volume objectives.

The attractive display—topped by a gingerbread house which could be awarded in a customer drawing— was surrounded by the participating products.

The cookbook used ingredients from all the participating companies. The recipe for kids faced a page on which kids could tell what they enjoyed most about baking, and win an Official Bakers Certificate.

When Dinosaurs
are the Thing

CLIENT:
Wendy's International Inc.,
Dublin, OH
(Tom Heskamp)

AGENCY:
Impact, Chicago
(Joseph P. Flanagan)

AWARDS:
1989 CSPA Award of Excellence
(Finalist)

Wendy's, third in the fast food hamburger field, has far less money to invest in promotion than #1 and #2, so it must make its dollars go farther. That's what this program did, basing its appeal on the heightened interest among children in those extinct reptiles called dinosaurs.

Until recently, Wendy's had never marketed to kids between two and 11. However, when real growth in the quick service restaurant industry began to flatten out in 1985, Wendy's recognized the need to broaden its regular customer base to include families with kids. This would be a way to steal market share from competitors.

The company had never ignored kids, since it had maintained a Kid's Meal program for the last four years. It had offered a small hamburger, fries, drink, and an inexpensive premium, all in a box. Now it felt was the time for upgrading, primarily increasing the quality and value of the premium included in the package.

Beginning in 1988, Wendy's offered a different package of premiums, each for a two-month period. Developed for the chain by Impact, the most successful of the first six of these promotions was the Definitely Dinosaurs Kids' Meal. This offered one of four available dinosaur figures —tyrannosaurus, Triceratops, apatosaurus, and anatosaurus—with each meal sold to a 3–9-year-old child. These were miniature editions of Playskool's popular toy line, produced exclusively for Wendy's. Comparable products would have sold for $1.99 to $2.99 at retail stores.

The summer of 1988 was a good one for a dinosaur promotion, because of the tremendous popularity of these animals, and the number of special exhibits being staged at museums, zoos, and so on during the summer. The tie-in with Hasbro's Playskool Division added weight to the impact of the promotion, since most parents and children were familiar with the line and accepted its value. Using four different dinosaurs provided an incentive to children to bring their families back to build their collection, and increase traffic during the promotion period.

Impact created all the supporting materials (including a four-color, sell-in brochure to describe the program), listed its costs to the individual store, and illustrated the merchandising and advertising support. A range of in-store point-of-purchase materials was created, including a large die-cut floor display, a dangler, and back-drop art for the permanent counter display. Special Kids' Meal box designs were also developed to support the premium offer, and a 30-second spot designed for Saturday morning television.

The promotion managed to increase the sale of Kids' Meal units by 28 per cent over the base period, with total restaurant sales up 7–9 percent, and traffic up 3–4 percent—significant figures in the highly competitive fast food business. It also was successful in blunting competitive promotion efforts targeted to kids. Some 40 percent more toy dinosaurs were distributed than originally projected, and Playskool was delighted with the higher levels of local broadcast support than they had expected.

An illuminated panel in the menu board couldn't be overlooked by customers.

Special placemats tied in with the promotion, giving the kids more information about dinosaurs.

The Way to the Heart

CLIENT:
Philip Morris USA; Marlboro
Cigarettes, New York
(Marla J. Antonoff, Nancy Lund)

AGENCY:
Leo Burnett, Chicago
(Allen Chichester)

An appeal to women often can center around their traditional skills of cooking. That's why this promotion proved to be very effective in getting women smokers to buy Marlboro cigarettes, in contrast with many earlier promotions for the brand, which tended to appeal to young adult males.

The immediate appeal was two-fold. Buyers of a carton of Marlboro cigarettes were offered a free cookbook of chuck wagon cooking, tying in with the outdoor, Western image of the cigarette. In addition, they got a $2 off coupon, but with a different twist. The $2 was given not for the purchase of the promoting brand, but on any other purchase made in the grocery store at that time! This had the advantage of being a good value to the consumer without discounting Marlboro.

Centerpiece of the promotion was a special display of a chuckwagon, loaded with 300 cartons of Marlboros! This was supported by shelf talkers directing customers to the display, by window banners, by 3' x 5' posters, and by hanging mobiles. At selected stores where the traffic was heavy enough, in-store cooking with sampling of a chili recipe added to the excitement. At other high-volume stores, there was a Marlboro Chuckwagon Cookin' Sweepstakes, featuring cooking activity.

The promotional elements provided in-store domination of the cigarette category and strong visibility for Marlboro. The incremental levels of carton volume were sold in and pulled through with this premium offer of a cookbook and a $2 grocery coupon. Exit interviews revealed that at least 20% of competitive smokers switched to Marlboro because of the promotion.

The added dimension of the in-store cooking demonstration, accompanied by Marlboro Country music, and the sweepstakes where it was held, created further excitement, interest and consumer involvement. The promotion resulted in a 2 percent increase in share during the promotional period. On a national basis, that amounts to an incremental 90 million packs!

A sheet from the folder described the live cooking demonstration that was made available in appropriate locations.

A four-color folder contains all the details of the promotion.

A New Way
to Handle Rebates

CLIENT:
Valvoline Oil Co., Lexington, KY
(John Stilwell)

AGENCY:
National Promotional Services,
Atlanta
(Daniel A. Dodson)

AWARDS:
1989 CSPA Award of Excellence
(Best of Category)

Historically, automotive aftermarket retailers have not accepted manufacturers' coupons, objecting to the long wait for redemption. As a result, price-off promotions in the form of rebates have bombarded many automarket categories, especially motor oil. This proliferation of rebates over time has led to a passive and stagnant retailer promotion attitude and mind-set. Furthermore, manufacturers' price-off wars were lowering Valvoline's margins and damaging profitability, since consumer rebate offers often reached as high as $5 off a $12 case of motor oil.

Valvoline was especially bothered by this, since it is the third largest selling motor oil in the country, and ranks number one in auto parts stores. Along with its sales promotion agency, it believed now was the time for a brand-new approach to the way Valvoline competed for retailer and consumer share-of-mind.

The challenge was clear. Rebates could no longer motivate the trade, and had become commonplace in the eyes of the consumer, while the technique of couponing was unaccepted in the automotive aftermarket. What was needed was a new price-off vehicle that would add value to a purchase of Valvoline, energize the trade, and excite the consumer.

The challenge was met with the development of the "Valvoline High Performance Check" promotion. Eighteen million checks made out to "Valvoline Retailers," each for $2, were inserted into popular consumer magazines, in the do-it-yourself and sports enthusiasts categories. These special checks could be used only toward the purchase of six or more quarts of Valvoline Motor Oil.

To the consumer, these checks worked like a coupon, giving him an instant discount at retailer locations, rather than forcing him to the trouble of mailing in a rebate form and waiting for his refund. The retailer, on the other hand, could deposit them immediately into his bank account, and redeem his discount immediately. This overcame the trade's objections with coupon redemption.

To add excitement to the consumer offer, and to further encourage trial, consumers also had the opportunity to win $100,000 by matching the number on the check to the number that was printed on the promotional point-of-sale display. This offer encouraged the dealer to set up the display when they came into the store. To avoid consumer disappointment, another $100,000 was offered in a second random draw sweepstakes, in which all consumers who missed the magazine inserts, or whose check number did not match, were entered.

The headlines on the consumer advertising read, "Win $100,000 Just for Changing Your Oil" while the trade headlines read "Here's a Promotion You Can Take to the Bank." Supporting the campaign was a complete promotional kit which included posters, shelf-talkers, entry blanks and ad slicks, as well as the header for the floor display. There were also inserts in consumer magazines, and advertising in the trade journals.

The promotion doubled Valvoline's previous record of displays installed, reaching record heights of 50,000 units! It surpassed sales goals, and cost only one-third as much as the activity in the same period the previous year. And while the change in dealers' attitudes toward Valvoline could not be measured, the company was bombarded with positive responses from both distributors and retailers.

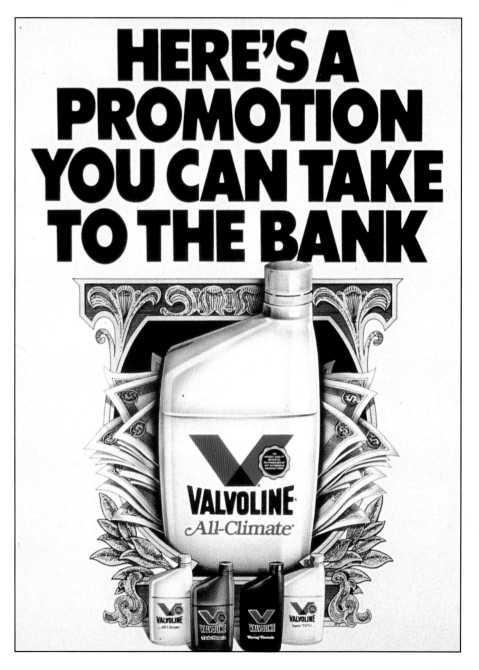

The consumer folder used the same bold type as the dealer one, but it showed the product in full color.

Riding an Event to Sales

CLIENT:
Captain Morgan Original Spiced
Rum/House of Seagram,
New York

AGENCY:
Siebel/Mohr, New York
(David Schendowich)

Captain Morgan Original Spiced Rum is a fun drink, with the average consumer of legal drinking age, of course, but under 34. It has a strong national franchise, with regional strengths in warm climates, beach areas and near colleges. Its brand image brings up thoughts of fun, excitement, and action.

That's why it seemed a good idea to tie promotion of the product with local events that added a touch of fun to the local scene. The first such event was in 1988, Gasparilla Day, held annually in Tampa on February 4. This is a day of pageantry and festivity, when it's time to relax and recollect the swashbuckling days of the pirates in the early history of the city. Exactly the right mood to lead a drinker to Captain Morgan's Original Spiced Rum!

And when he went looking for fun, whether in liquor stores or in taverns, he found displays of the Seagram brand, with a supply of sweepstakes/scratch cards. Each contained an area to be scratched off to reveal either "Winner" or "Try Again." Winners could take their cards to a central location and claim their prize on the spot. There were more than a thousand winning cards printed and distributed. Six hundred of them could win a Captain Morgan Hat and 400 a T-shirt imprinted with

Captain Morgan in honor of Gasparilla Day. There were 20 first prizes of dinner for two, and a single grand prize of $2,500 in cash. If the holder of a winning card couldn't or didn't want to make it to the central location to claim his prize, he could mail in his card and get his prize by mail. And even if the card was a loser, the holder could be entered in a seocnd chance drawing, by signing his card and mailing it to the second chance address. If any of the winning cards weren't turned in, the remaining prizes would be distributed in a drawing among second chance cards.

All sweepstakes cards had a coupon to be sent in if the holder wanted to purchase the special Captain Morgan T-Shirt, which required a proof-of-purchase plus a cash payment.

The promotion was supported by newspaper advertising, both nationally funded, and by inclusion in retail store ads. On-premise drink nights, with special bar kits and visits from Captain Morgan and his crew, added excitement to the local scene. For retail stores, there was a display competition to help achieve installations.

The promotion was further tested at the 1988 celebration of Patriots Day, in Boston in April, and again at the 1989 Gasparilla Day. All regional volume and distribution objectives were surpassed at these events, and six more were added to the schedule:

- Patriots Day, April 1989, Boston
- Billy Bowlegs Day, April 1989, Key West
- Contraband Days, May 1989, Lake Charles, LA
- Bastille Day, July 1989, Milwaukee
- Port Huron to Mackinack, MI, Boat Race, July 1989
- Stamford Sailboat Show, Sept. 1989, Stamford, TC

The colorful stack header was keyed to the local event.

It's Chicken to Challenge

CLIENT:
Hygrade Chicken Products,
Detroit
(Margaret Riley)

AGENCY:
Davidson Marketing, Chicago
(Russell Blanchard, Tom Baer, Virginia
Van Cleve, Chuck Shotwell)

When Hygrade was about to introduce a broad new line of chicken products, which included such items as chicken franks, chicken bologna and chicken cotto salami, it knew it had to do something to counteract the natural tendency to stick to the old and familiar. It was, of course, a healthy alternative to similar beef products, but simple health considerations do not always lead to a change in habits.

What was needed was something that would get people to move, and Davdison Marketing created "The Grillmaster Challenge" to achieve this goal. The challenge was put before the consumer in a full page, free-standing insert, as well as at point-of-purchase displays, offering them a refund of $1.50 if they didn't prefer Grillmaster to their regular brand. Pads of tear-off coupons permitted customers to file their requests for refunds.

This was supported by local promotions which featured a series of "real people" turning chicken by substituting a Grillmaster product for the comparable one made of beef. Each of these offers, made on a p-o-p display, offered some incentive, like a can of soup, with a purchase of a chicken product.

The promotion to the trade extended the same theme to store personnel. It used a series of inserts, each based on a typical person, like Cora the Cashier, or Benny the Bagger, each of whom was turning chicken. The campaign featured a mystery shopper program that offered key account representatives an opportunity to win up to $5,000 in cash.

The tongue-in-cheek approach got its story across without being heavy-handed, and got retailers to feature the new line, and customers to try it, with a remarkably low number of demands from customers to get their $1.50 back.

Portfolio inserts used the same design, and carried on the theme of the mythical figures who were turning chicken. The selection of inserts was made on the intended audiences.

Counter cards were built around people, with a now-familiar layout. Each offered a different product with a Grillmaster purchase, and included a coupon pad.

chapter SIX

Jan Soderstrom
Vice President, Advertising
Visa USA

Integrate Promotion, Advertising, and Sales Promotion

In today's world of parity products, promotions are more important than ever. Especially when your goal is to build and sustain brand loyalty, or increase usage of your product.

Smart marketers begin with a vision that unifies their marketing goals—and dollars—into integrated promotion, advertising and public relations campaigns. Synergistic campaigns are not only more impactful, but they also deliver more results for every dollar spent.

And speaking of cost effectiveness, don't overlook your own backyard. It's always easier (and far less expensive) to encourage your customers to increase usage of your product than it is to win new customers. Think about it. You know a lot about the buying habits and demographic profile of your current customers. You have an idea of what kind of promotional tactic will spark their interest, and what will leave them cold. And that's half the battle already won.

Gold Picks Up the Check

CLIENT:
Visa USA, San Mateo, CA
(Jan Soderstrom)

AGENCY:
Frankel & Company, Chicago
(Joanne Belle, Colleen Fahey)

AWARDS:
1989 CSPA Award of Excellence
(Finalist)

How do you run a nationwide promotion without getting in the way of up to 480 other promotions aimed at the same audiences? With the help of its sales promotion agency, Visa USA found a way.

Visa had just reintroduced its Gold Card, and it needed to give consumers a compelling reason to choose it over other cards, especially American Express which had historically dominated the Travel and Entertainment market. It needed a major impact, but it didn't want to step on the toes of its member financial institutions, who were issuing the cards, many of whom were running their own promotions. What's more, a national promotion had to be open to all Visa Gold cardholders, of whom there were 8,000,000, without significantly interfering with issuers' operations.

Visa adopted the idea of offering to pick up the check for its cardholders. During a pre-specified period, Visa selected purchases at random, and paid for them by issuing credits on the cardholder's account. There was a maximum of $75,000 on the purchase to be paid for, and the total amount of the checks picked up by Visa would not exceed one million dollars. Visa would keep on treating its customers as long as the money held out, or until December 31, whichever came earlier.

The headline on the mailing piece to cardholders read "Use Visa Gold and your purchase could be on us. It's Our Treat." The sales promotion agency also prepared a member involvement mailing and training materials for the personnel at issuing institutions to inform them about the promotion. Statement inserts helped keep cardholder interest alive, and posters and displays to be installed in branch offices reached non-cardholders as well. The agency also took charge of implementing the sweepstakes, supervising the processing of winning purchase selections, notifying winners, and handling all telephone contact with consumers and trade.

To intensify the excitement, and to encourage large purchases, Visa had an additional monthly drawing to pick up three cardholders each month, and pay off their previous month's account balance up to $100,000.

During the promotion period, Visa transactions were 58 percent higher. However, since the general market trend was up, and since there were other promotional efforts run at the same time by card issuers, it is not possible to establish how much of this increase could be attributed to this promotion. It obviously satisfied

member banks, since their orders for point-of-purchase materials exceeded projections by 800 per cent, and Visa planned to expand the promotion in 1989 to include its entire card base of 110 million cardholders.

The brochure that explained the promotion to member financial institutions held a specially-made videotape to add to the excitement.

A poster was designed to go up on members' premises where a cardholder would see it.

A folder that explained the promotion was sent out to all cardholders, generally with their monthly statements.

Self- Promotion Sells

CLIENT/AGENCY:
Berenson, Isham & Partners Inc.,
Boston
(Paul Berenson)

AWARDS:
Target Marketing Magazine
New England Direct Marketing
Association
Art Direction Magazine

If direct mail is your specialty, then you should use direct mail to sell yourself. That's the theory that has been adopted by Boston direct response and sales promotion agency, Berenson, Isham & Partners Inc. It has developed a careful and impressive campaign to tell prospects about itself.

It starts, as all direct mail campaigns must do, with building the mailing list of target companies, and within those, the key executive responsible for advertising and direct marketing is identified. While the detailed criteria are cards kept close to the chest, these target companies must obviously be large enough to afford the kind of campaign the agency does best, have a product or a sales goal which can use direct response techniques, and have a corporate philosophy which is sympathetic to that of the agency.

Three posters form the nucleus of the program. These are in full color, on fine coated paper, each 18" x 24". The posters are based on a series of stamps issued by the U.S. Postal Service during our nation's bicentennial. A series of white dots immediately suggest direct mail advertising.

The first mailing contains the poster whose headline is "Revolutionary direct mail ideas for under 31." A personal letter, signed by the agency's Vice President of Business Development, amplifies the copy on the poster. Shortly thereafter, the recipient is reached by telephone and qualified. The results of this contact can be as encouraging as an immediate appointment to discuss a project, or as disappointing as a demand to be removed immediately from the mailing list. Most of the responses fall between these two, and the campaign, which can last several months, continues.

The second poster, headlined "When it comes to direct marketing, we run a very tight ship," uses the familiar painting of Washington crossing the Delaware. It, too, is accompanied by a personal covering letter and is followed up with a telephone call.

The third mailing in the series is a change of pace. It is a 16-page booklet, 8½"x 11", that tells the agency story by describing earlier campaigns, for specific clients, that the agency has developed and carried out. In addition to direct mail, these case histories indicate the use of direct response space and broadcast advertising as well.

The fourth set mailing returns to the poster motif, this time using the one with the headline "Behind every great piece of copy there's always a big idea," under the illustration of the signing of the Declaration of Independence.

While these four mailings are the nucleus of the campaign, the program is flexible, so both the timing and the contents of mailings

can be adjusted to meet whatever interests of the prospects develop during his contacts with the agency. Samples of current or recent efforts supplement the series.

The brochure uses fine photography —in full color on glossy paper—to impart an air of top quality.

Telemarketing + Mail = Winner

CLIENT:
MCI Telecommunications Inc.,
Washington, DC

AGENCY:
The Carlson Marketing Group,
Minneapolis
(Mary Wathen)

A straightforward campaign developed by the Carlson Marketing Group for MCI Telecommunications succeeded in breaking through in a situation where all suppliers are perceived as being approximately equal in services, and thus prospects are amenable to a special price promotion.

And that's what MCI offered prospects. For a small monthly charge, it offered new customers one hour's free calling on evenings and weekends, and a 10 percent discount on calls made at other times. This would be a three-month trial of MCI, after which the user had the option of continuing on the standard relationship, paying only for whatever calls were made.

To introduce this offer, MCI offered a list of prospects, and called each to explain the program. No attempt was made to sign up people on this initial call. The pitch was directed to getting the prospect to ask for an explanatory brochure. This was not a difficult thing to do, since the prospect did not have to agree to anything that cost money, just to accept a piece of mail.

But subconsciously, commitment of any sort is the first step toward a sale, so that when the offer arrived in the mail, it was expected, and response was excellent.

The mailing piece itself was simple, consisting of a cover letter, a business reply envelope, and a four-color brochure which explained the details of the offer. A return coupon was part of the cover letter, but there was also an 800 number for those who wanted quicker action.

It was a simple operation, but the results, greater than expectations, proved that if you have a good offer, professionally offered, you can achieve good results.

Reduce. Drop. Trim. Cut.
No matter what word you use, Prime Time promises to get your long distance bills down by as much as 32%!

Hello:

Recently, you spoke with one of our MCI marketing representatives and expressed an interest in the MCI Prime Time Offer.* It's a great introduction to the savings and service you'll experience as an MCI long distance customer.

Enclosed is the Prime Time brochure you requested. Please take a moment to read it and learn more about the advantages of Prime Time.

For a full three months—for only $6.00 a month—you'll enjoy:

• A full hour's worth of night and weekend calling.*

• An additional 10% discount off MCI's already low rates on both in-state and out-of-state, direct dial calls.

• The convenience, simplicity and uncompromising quality of MCI long distance service.

To take advantage of this Prime Time introductory offer, we must hear from you right away! Simply return the attached reply form in the postage-paid envelope provided. Or, for faster service, give us a call at **1-800-444-3333**.

There's never been a better time to trim excess costs off your long distance bills.

Sincerely,

Wayne R. Thomas
Director of Consumer Services

P.S. Remember, this is a limited time offer—sign up for Prime Time right away!

*Your full hour's worth of calling will be given in the form of a credit. The credit will equal an amount up to $8.09, MCI's charge for a one hour domestic call in the 1911-3000 mileage band at night/weekend rates. Offer valid to non-MCI customers only in California, Nevada and Hawaii where MCI Dial "1" service is available. One MCI Prime Time Offer per customer account. Offer expires March 31, 1989.

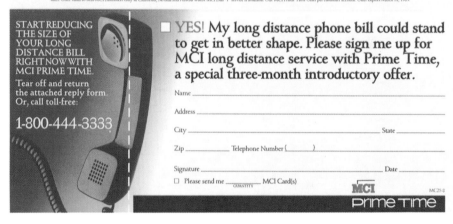

YES! My long distance phone bill could stand to get in better shape. Please sign me up for MCI long distance service with Prime Time, a special three-month introductory offer.

START REDUCING THE SIZE OF YOUR LONG DISTANCE BILL RIGHT NOW WITH MCI PRIME TIME.

Tear off and return the attached reply form. Or, call toll-free:

1-800-444-3333

Name _____
Address _____
City _____ State _____
Zip _____ Telephone Number ( ) _____
Signature _____ Date _____
☐ Please send me _____ MCI Card(s)

MC25-8

Prime Time

Here's the Prime Time 90-day plan to a slimmer long distance bill.

MCI
Let us show you.

MC25-6

© MCI Communications Corporation 1989

With your full hour's worth of night and weekend calling, you get gain with no pain.

You'll save up to 32% vs. AT&T when you use this full hour of night and weekend calling for out-of-state direct dial calls.*

And now it's easier than ever to stay in touch with friends and family. Prime Time provides you with 60 minutes of no-charge night and weekend calls to anywhere in the U.S. every month for your first three months as an MCI customer.

Nighttime and weekends always seem to be a good time to reach people at home and for you to relax and enjoy a phone call. So by making your calls during these times, you can take full advantage of your 60 minutes worth of monthly calling credit.

*Your full hour's worth of calling will be given in the form of a credit. The credit will equal an amount up to $8.09, MCI's charge for a one hour domestic call in the 1911-3000 mileage band at night/weekend rates. Offer valid to non-MCI customers only in California, Nevada and Hawaii where MCI Dial "1" service is available. One MCI Prime Time Offer per customer account. Offer expires March 31, 1989.

You'll trim 10% more off MCI's low rates on all domestic, direct dial calls to anywhere in the U.S.

With Prime Time you can reduce cost without reducing your calls.

In fact, you'll save an additional 10% off MCI's already low rates on all of your direct dial calls—both in and out of state…whenever you call–day, night AND weekends. Get ready to enjoy what could be the best calling discount available anywhere!

Prime Time gives you a three-month start on a leaner long distance bill.

For only $6.00 a month, you'll enjoy the benefits of Prime Time for a full three months. A great introduction to the service and savings you'll receive as an MCI customer.

At the end of the three-month introductory period, you will be an MCI Dial "1" customer and continue to benefit from the service and call quality MCI is famous for! And, you'll continue to save on every call vs. AT&T's standard out-of-state rates. You will no longer pay a $6.00 monthly charge and will be billed at our low Dial "1" rates for each call you make.

In addition to providing you with unequaled value, MCI is easy to use. You can call from any phone, any time to anywhere in the world you can dial direct. Just dial "1," the area code and the phone number. There are no access or authorization codes or extra digits to remember.

And when you travel, take MCI's great quality and value with you with the MCI Card.*

All in all, MCI offers you an easy way to maintain your new, slimmer long distance phone bill.

Exercise your good judgement. Sign-up for Prime Time today!

Simply return the Prime Time reply form attached to the enclosed letter.

Or, for faster service, call our toll free number: **1-800-444-3333**.

MCI Customer Service representatives are available to take your call 24 hours a day, 365 days a year.

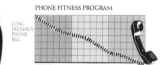

PHONE FITNESS PROGRAM

LONG DISTANCE PHONE BILL

BEFORE   AFTER

Call **1-800-444-3333** today!

MCI
Prime Time

A Landmark Promotion

CLIENT:
American Express, New York

AGENCY:
Comart-KLP, New York
(Lori F. Brandon)

AWARDS:
1989 CSPA Award of Excellence
(Finalist)

The leading travelers check in the United States is issued by American Express. In this volatile market environment, consumer awareness and product loyalty remain high. This has led American Express to focus on trade programs as an overall travelers check promotional technique. Trade promotions have proven to be effective in generating top-of-mind awareness in tellers, and this stimulates sales. In addition, an active promotion program helps to build and strengthen existing account relationships and aids in obtaining new accounts. The total dollar sales volume of the product is large, and therefore the slightest increase in sales for the market leader is significant.

In the past, American Express promotions were small, and each targeted to a specific account. This led to inefficiencies in cost and required inordinate amounts of administration. For 1988, the company decided to achieve economies by offering a national promotion targeted to a larger base of priority accounts.

Since the general marketing strategy was to emphasize domestic travel, the theme "American Landmarks" seemed an especially appropriate one, and the promotion technique selected was a straightforward sweepstakes. Each time a teller sold

American Express Travelers Cheques, he or she was entitled to complete and send in an entry form. The more sold, the greater the chance of winning a prize.

More than 31,000 prizes were awarded in the three-month promotion, with a drawing taking place each month. This frequency kept interest and enthusiasm high. The grand prize—and there were 10 of them—was a 2-week vacation, plus $1,000 in travelers checks. This was followed by 25 Sylvania camcorders, 50 Sharp VCRs, 100 Sony CD players, 1,000 $25 American Express gift checks, and 30,000 pocket cameras.

Some 6,000 institutions all over the country were invited to participate in the sweepstakes, and about 2,000 of them agreed, accounting for 19,000 locations and more than 152,000 tellers. When the deadline for participation had passed, a promotion kit was sent to each of the locations specified by the financial institutions. In addition to the entry blanks which would be used by the tellers, the kit contained an American Landmarks poster which would be used in places like employees' lounges, to keep the promotion up front.

This poster was used to get the promotion off to a quick start, and to make sure that all tellers were aware of it. One of the elements of the kit was an inexpensive flash camera. The branch was asked to use the camera to take a photo of all the tellers around the poster. The first 100 photos received by American Express won a $25 Travelers Cheque for each teller at the location. This was a way of ensuring that all tellers knew about the promotion, and it was evident from the photos received, that they were anxious to take part.

Over 7,000 of these "Quick Start" photos were received, and more than 650,000 sweepstakes entries. Sales at the 2,000 participating institutions were approximately 6.84 percent higher than at the non-participating ones.

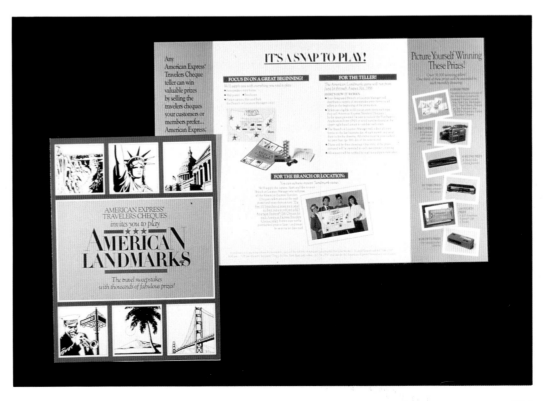

Each participating location got a large poster which, when posted in employee lounges, served as a constant reminder of the prizes that awaited the winners.

Direct Mail
Solves a Problem

CLIENT:
Northwest Airlines, Minneapolis

AGENCY:
The Carlson Marketing Group,
Minneapolis
(Mary Wathen)

The frequent flyer program has been successful in building repeat business with a particular airline, and many airlines, including Northwest Air, have found this a useful promotional technique. But frequent flyer miles that are not used within a reasonable time become somewhat of a threat. Not only would the airline like to see its customers enjoy the benefits of the travel they have earned, but it would also like to get rid of the accounting figure it must carry to cover redemption of the free travel.

To get rid of this mileage liability, Northwest and its sales promotion agency, Carlson Marketing Group, set up a plan to offer trips to attractive places at a discount, and at a time when planes were flying to those places not fully loaded. The two offers covered travel to Europe and the Caribbean, in which a traveler could get a free trip for only 20,000 miles, instead of the normal 40,000.

Colorful leaflets were prepared, outlining the offer. Each was good for a limited period: the Caribbean in September 1988 only, and the European between November 1, 1988 and March 1, 1989. The European offer was not available during the Thanksgiving or the Christmas/New Year holiday periods.

These mailers went out with monthly statements to WORLDPERKS members. Those who wished to take advantage of this special offer made their reservations directly, in the normal way. Thus the promotion added no special burden to the airline's staff. They simply issued tickets, within the limitations set by the offer, but accepted only half the mileage during the promotion period.

The promotion worked exactly as it had been planned. The inserts generated so many tickets that the available inventory was liquidated. And best of all, since the promotion was offered on flights that had excess capacity, the outstanding mileage was wiped out at no cost to the airline.

These colorful folders, 8½"x3⅝", succeeded in getting flyers with free mileage due to redeem for flights that otherwise would be filled with empty seats.

AGENCY INDEX

CLIENT INDEX

AWARDS INDEX

DIRECT MARKETING DESIGN 2

DIRECT MARKETING DESIGN 2 vividly displays the newest ideas and techniques of the direct mail industry. In 248 full-color pages, the winners of the prestigious John Caples Awards are clearly presented. This competition is sponsored by the Direct Marketing Creative Guild, and is judged by a panel of direct marketing experts from all levels of the industry. Brief descriptions that include the designers' intent accompany each of the 270 illustrations. DIRECT MARKETING DESIGN 2 is a fabulous reference tool to all in the fields of direct mail, advertising, public relations and marketing. Many topics graphically present excellence in direct marketing creativity and design including:

- Direct mail for consumers
- Direct mail for business to business
- Print advertising for consumers and business-to-business
- Collateral Material
- Multimedia and single media direct response campaigns

248 pages, 9″ x 12″
Over 300 illustrations
ISBN 0-86636-061-1
$60.00

Hundreds of award-winning designs fill the 248 pages of this 9″ x 12″ idea sourcebook. Captions and chapter openers accompany the direct mail pieces and describe what is the special facet, that unique "something" that makes each piece a winner!

STAND OUT FROM THE REST. ORDER YOUR COPY TODAY!

FOR ORDER INFORMATION PLEASE SEE ORDER FORM ON THE BACK JACKET.